T0246262

SWING HARD
IN CASE YOU HIT IT

SWING HARD
IN CASE YOU HIT IT

My Escape from Addiction
and Shot at Redemption
on the Trump Campaign

TIM MURTAUGH

BOMBARDIER
BOOKS

Published by Bombardier Books
An Imprint of Post Hill Press

Swing Hard in Case You Hit It:
My Escape from Addiction and Shot at Redemption on the Trump Campaign
© 2024 by Tim Murtaugh
All Rights Reserved

ISBN: 979-8-88845-324-7
ISBN (eBook): 979-8-88845-325-4

Cover design by Conroy Accord

This is a work of nonfiction. All people, locations, events, and situations are portrayed to the best of the author's memory.

Post Hill Press
New York • Nashville
posthillpress.com

Published in the United States of America
2 3 4 5 6 7 8 9 10

PREFACE

This book will probably be unlike any other you've read by someone in politics. It has some stories from inside the Trump 2020 presidential re-election campaign, but it's not totally about that race, or Donald J. Trump, for that matter.

It's about the path that I took, starting early in life, and the poor choices that I made that eventually threatened to ruin everything I had tried to achieve over my first forty-five years on this planet. It's about going to jail—twice—because I couldn't stop guzzling alcohol, and it's about very nearly losing my loving wife, my career, and all my self-respect, and still somehow recovering to hold a prominent job for the president of the United States less than four years later.

It's also about some of my political life after I quit drinking. In the following pages, you'll read about some of my experiences as the communications director for the Trump 2020 campaign, some good and some bad. But unlike a lot of political books of this era, it won't be about bashing Donald Trump or making headlines by spilling juicy gossip. I am proud to have worked for President Trump, and proud to have run comms on his re-election campaign. To have been trusted with that responsibility remains the highest honor of my professional career, but that's not to say that all the campaign stories contained herein are happy ones. Far from it, in fact.

So, this is a redemption story, I suppose, although according to many people on Twitter I am well beyond hope for that because I worked for Trump. But it's also a story about someone—me—who had to be battered about the head with the same lessons, over and over and over, until one day they finally registered, when I was faced with no other choice. So, redemption, yes, but it took an awfully long time and, at least professionally, it wasn't exactly the perfect ending. Either way, while writing the first draft of the manuscript for this book I marked eight years since my last drink.

It's also a cautionary tale, because I bet there are many people, in politics or not, who can read my story and see much of themselves in the ridiculous and self-sabotaging behavior in which I engaged for too many years. I know from my own experience that each time I was in rehab (yes, I went multiple times), I was a regular at the bookstore, buying and devouring all the titles that were more biographical than clinical. I much preferred reading about the real struggles that people experienced and how they made it through them, and I'm sure there are many other alcoholics who feel the same way.

My incredibly helpful, dedicated, and forgiving wife, Dena Kozanas, first encouraged me to write a book of this nature several years ago. It always sounded like a good idea, but I never thought I'd really do it. Dena is a private person and doesn't relish these details becoming public, but at the same time she knows that it's a story that can possibly help other people. She witnessed much of my personal war with alcohol, and I can state unequivocally and without exaggeration that without her in my life I would either be in jail or dead today. I know that she has suffered greatly as well and continues to be haunted by memories of how I used to be, a reminder that the people closest to active alcoholics often have it worse than the alcoholics themselves. It was imperative that she was on board with my writing this book, and I think it's good that she was, because I believe she turns out to be the hero of the story.

In some ways, this book is a defense-by-offense move for me, because telling on myself in this way means that I've revealed it on my terms, and my past will no longer have the power that dark secrets sometimes have. I have consciously not included every episode that I might, because as alcoholics in recovery, we're not supposed to unburden ourselves of these things if there's the potential to hurt other people by bringing them up.

I truly hope that reading about what I went through can help another alcoholic to get closer to being sober. I know that writing it all down for once certainly helped me to continue to avoid drinking, one day at a time, because I was reminded of how farcical my whole existence once was. But I don't think that you have to be a drunk to appreciate the stories in here, or to just shake your head.

The way I decided to go about writing this book is with two different timelines, one during my drinking days and the other after I had dried out, which was less than four years before I joined the Trump campaign. This made sense to me because they were really two different lives—the drinking me versus the sober me—and the story alternates between the two, with a shot glass graphic noting my drinking status at the beginning of each chapter.

While I was writing, I tried to follow the advice my father always gave me before baseball practice: "Swing hard in case you hit it." That's good counsel for all aspects of life, if you think about it, and it's what I'm trying to do with this book.

Anyway, here's my story.

Tim Murtaugh
Leesburg, Virginia, September 2023

INTRODUCTION

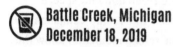 **Battle Creek, Michigan**
December 18, 2019

A week before Christmas 2019, it was a bitterly cold Wednesday night in Battle Creek, Michigan, windy with temperatures in the teens most of the day. Inside Kellogg Arena, a multi-purpose facility with a capacity listed at 6,200, thousands of supporters of President Donald J. Trump filled the seats to the rafters and flooded the floor in front of the stage that would be the epicenter of the coming rally. As they awaited what everyone suspected would be an especially fiery Trump speech, the crowd rocked out to the pre-rally playlist and kept the arena warm through body heat.

It would soon get hotter.

The Trump 2020 campaign road show had roared into town on that night, like it had in so many other places on so many other nights, but this time it was different. This time, the president of the United States was going to be impeached by the House of Representatives back in Washington, DC, at roughly the same time that he was expected to step up to the microphone in Michigan.

Except there was uncertainty backstage, where I stood with President Trump, Vice President Mike Pence, and a variety of senior officials from the White House and re-election campaign. A monitor was tuned to Fox News, which showed the live feed from the House floor at the Capitol. A determination had to be made: Should Trump begin speaking as scheduled, or should he wait for the final votes before going on stage?

Waiting for the votes to conclude carried risk, as far as the timing of the rally went, because there was no telling how long the voting would take, and it was not reasonable to delay the president's remarks indefinitely.

Yet, if Trump took the stage while the vote was underway, it was unclear how the news of the result would reach him mid-speech.

Some in the media had theorized that the Trump campaign had engineered this made-for-television split-screen moment. I know this, because I had become the communications director for the president's re-election campaign in February of that year, and I had heard the speculation. To be fair, it seemed like classic Trump showmanship, to beg coverage of his defiant remarks to raucous supporters juxtaposed with the solemn images from the House chamber. But the truth was that the rally had been planned and scheduled well before anyone knew when Speaker Nancy Pelosi would schedule the impeachment votes. It was more likely that Pelosi had set the date and time of the votes with the rally in mind.

Regardless, the fact remained that the Trump speech and the impeachment votes were on a collision course, timing-wise.

There was discussion backstage among President Trump, campaign manager Brad Parscale, White House advisor Stephen Miller, and others, including Vice President Mike Pence, who also had made the trip to Michigan for this important night. As someone who was relatively new to the higher rungs of Trump World at the time, I mostly watched, listened, and just tried to take in every aspect of what was clearly a monumental night in American history.

I quietly took a few pictures of the scene with my phone as the decision was made: Trump would take the stage and we would send someone out to signal him with the news when the vote was final.

The familiar strains of Lee Greenwood's "God Bless the USA," Trump's signature entrance music, blared from the loudspeakers. The president of the United States made his slow approach to the lectern, stopping periodically, waving to his fans, pointing to individuals in the crowd, and clapping along with them. This was quintessential Trump—milking every second of his walk-up song and delighting the thousands of screaming supporters.

Once he arrived at the microphone, he got rolling and didn't waste any time before tearing into Pelosi and the Democrats in Washington.

"Crazy Nancy Pelosi's House Democrats have branded themselves with an eternal mark of shame," Trump told the roaring crowd. "It's a disgrace."

"After three years of sinister witch hunts, hoaxes, and scams, tonight the House Democrats are trying to nullify the ballots of tens of millions of patriotic Americans," Trump said, accusing Democrats of "interfering in America's elections" and "subverting American democracy."

At this exact moment, the House was voting to impeach him on two counts involving his dealings with Ukraine, accusing him of abusing his power to pressure the Ukrainian president to investigate Democratic candidate Joe Biden and then obstructing congressional investigations of the matter.

I stood backstage, simply marveling at the very fact that I was present for the historic event and watching the silent television feed of the impeachment proceedings with the vice president standing immediately to my right. In front of us, behind the monitor, rose a broad and tall black curtain separating us from the bowl of the arena. On the other side of the pipe and drape rigging, the man who would soon be impeached was delivering the speech that was meant to harness

Republican anger at the development and turn it into a potent campaign weapon.

The air felt heavy with the gravity of the simultaneous events. And for me, to experience it standing next to the vice president on one side of the curtain while listening to the president speak from the other, it was a true "remember where you were" moment, and I was right there where it was all happening.

When the voting was finished, the House had impeached Trump on both counts. On the charge of abuse of power, the vote was 230 in favor to 197 against, with two Democrats—Collin Peterson and Jeff Van Drew—siding with all Republicans, and another Democrat, Tulsi Gabbard, voting "present." On the charge of obstructing Congress, the vote was 229 in favor to 198 against, with three Democrats—Peterson, Van Drew, and Jared Golden—siding with all Republicans, and Gabbard voting "present" again.

And now the word had to get to Trump, who had worked the crowd into a full lather.

White House deputy press secretary Hogan Gidley, who would leave the administration to join the Trump re-election campaign in June 2020, began assembling a large sign to alert Trump to the news. With White House press secretary Stephanie Grisham observing, Gidley used equipment in a makeshift office area to print large numbers on individual pieces of paper, which he then affixed to a large posterboard. Understanding that this one-way communication to the president on stage had to be succinct, Gidley's poster would only describe one of the two impeachment votes, and he chose the second one because a larger number of Democrats had defected to support Trump.

The finished product had two lines of numbers.

The first line read, "229-198"—referring to the breakdown of yeas and nays.

The second line simply read, "3"—referring to the number of Democrats who had defected to oppose the impeachment.

The method of delivery seemed obvious, and the task was given to campaign press secretary Kayleigh McEnany, who would later leave the campaign to become White House press secretary, replacing Grisham, in April 2020.

Tall with long blonde hair, wearing a bright orange dress, and recognizable to Trump by sight, McEnany would be easy to spot in the buffer area between the front of the stage and the crowd. She walked out from the backstage area and took a position in front of Trump and slightly to his left, holding the sign in front of her so he could easily see it.

"Oh, I think we have a vote coming in," Trump said, immediately spotting McEnany. "So, we got every single Republican voted for us. Whoa, wow, wow. Almost 200. So, we had 198, 229, 198. We didn't lose one Republican vote and, and three Democrats voted for us."

That's the story of how the forty-fifth president of the United States learned that he had become just the third president in history to be impeached. As the rally concluded—after a speech that timed out to be his longest rally speech to that point at just over two hours—the feeling inside the campaign was that the impeachment would ultimately work in the president's favor politically. The charges were flimsy and transparently partisan.

The campaign had long believed that the Democrats were over-reaching—that they could be easily depicted as DC elitists attempting to thwart the will of the people, who strongly supported Trump's policies. If, as expected, the Senate acquitted Trump of the charges (as it would do on February 5, 2020), the impeachment would be used to galvanize his supporters and cast the entire election as the "Washington swamp" pitted against normal, everyday citizens.

At the time, we couldn't have known that this would only be the first of two impeachments of President Donald J. Trump, or that a global pandemic would strike just a few months later, prompting lockdowns, school closures, and economic calamity, and eventually killing more than a million Americans.

The COVID-19 plague that swept the planet completely disrupted the campaign and became the undeniable top issue, dwarfing impeachments and any other topic, canceling rallies and most public events, and allowing eventual Democratic nominee Joe Biden to avoid public appearances and largely campaign from his basement in Wilmington, Delaware.

We couldn't have known that a laptop owned by Biden's son, Hunter, would surface to reveal information that tied the father to the son's influence-peddling schemes involving foreign moneymen, or that social media platforms and the national news media would combine to suppress the story as the campaign drew to a close in November 2020.

We couldn't have known that an unruly mob would storm the US Capitol on January 6, 2021, as Congress met to certify a Biden victory, leading to that second impeachment and another acquittal.

And we couldn't have known that the election of 2020 would drag on for years beyond Election Day, with the congressional January 6 Committee investigation and hearings and a subsequent Department of Justice investigation and grand jury.

None of those things was knowable seven days before Christmas 2019, when it seemed like the events of December 18 would resonate and dominate for the length of the campaign.

What I did know was that for me, personally, the experience that night in Battle Creek was exhilarating. I had spent many years in politics, on campaigns and with political committees at the state and national levels, but that impeachment night rally was not something I had ever expected to witness from inside the inner bubble at a presidential event. For someone involved in political communications as a career, this was the top of the professional mountain; it's not an exaggeration to say that the 2020 American presidential election was the most watched political campaign in world history, and I was the communications director for the incumbent.

But I felt like an unlikely participant, and the feeling was especially strong because, not many years earlier, I had been on a decidedly different—and destructive and dangerous—path. Not long before that night in Battle Creek, I had been in another situation that was difficult for entirely different reasons.

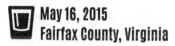

May 16, 2015
Fairfax County, Virginia

When I began to come to, I knew I was in trouble before I even opened my eyes.

There was the familiar feeling of fogginess, the awareness that I had gotten impossibly drunk again, and the immediate rush of shame for letting it happen once more. But it all came with recognizable additions—the institutional vibrations and atmosphere of my physical surroundings—and that presented a bigger problem. I knew what it meant because I'd been in such places before.

A dull ache in the back of my head told me that I was lying on a hard floor, and I could tell that I had my feet propped up on a hard chair of some kind. My hands found my face and I felt around for fresh wounds or blood (injuries had happened in the past) and, finding none, I opened my eyes.

I've heard it said in the rooms of Alcoholics Anonymous that, often, we problem drinkers don't wake up from sleeping one off as much as we "come to," and that's exactly what happened to me that day.

I sat up, still on the floor, and took it in: a holding room in what was certainly a police station. There were rows of plastic chairs joined together by armrests to prevent anyone from lying down across several seats, which was evidently why I had been passed out with my head on the floor. Bolted to the ceiling was a television somewhat loudly playing a program I don't recall today.

Around me, other men were engaged in various methods of doing nothing. Some slumped awkwardly in the chairs, some slept, some watched TV. Still others stood at the one wall that consisted mostly of Plexiglas windows and looked out into a common area of some kind. Almost no one in the room was talking, as far as I could tell.

I decided to risk standing up.

Using the row of plastic chairs to steady myself, I rose to my feet to test my equilibrium. Once upright, I walked over to the wall of windows without incident. I could see another, larger room on the other side of the partition. There were cops out there. Lots of them. Some looked like they were doing paperwork, and some were interviewing sad-looking people who would probably be joining us in the smaller room shortly.

For some reason I felt compelled to reach with my hand to feel my pockets, knowing what I would find—rather, what I would not find—as the case was. My wallet was missing. I patted both front pockets. No cell phone. Looking down, I saw that my shoes were gone as well. And, lifting my shirt, I discovered that I was beltless also.

There was a guy standing near me by the window. "Where are we?" I asked him.

"Fairfax," he said.

"Fairfax what?"

"Fairfax County jail," he said, and moved away.

I didn't feel hungover yet because I was undoubtedly still quite drunk, but I thought sitting down for a while would feel much better than standing. As I found a spot on a hard plastic chair, I tried to take stock of what I knew.

I had quite clearly been arrested, no doubt for an alcohol-related offense. I was being held in a large holding room in what I would learn was the Adult Detention Center at the Fairfax County Judicial Center. I wasn't wearing handcuffs, but all my personal belongings had been confiscated. At least I wasn't injured.

I also was not panicked, because I had been in similar situations before. It's not something to be proud of, but the fact that I'd been arrested before probably helped me to stay calm while I assessed my situation. There was a booth toward the back of the room that contained a pay phone, but there wasn't anyone I was brave enough to call just yet.

A sudden realization hit me, and I sat bolt upright in the plastic chair, feeling real shock register. I mean, I could feel it through my arms and into my fingers, down my legs and into my feet, like a real electrical jolt. Some synapses had fired, and I had made the connection between this arrest and one of my other ones.

I was in serious trouble. More than ever before, for sure.

Because of an earlier DUI conviction (my second), I had served ten days in jail and was still on probation, with eighty days of suspended jail time hanging over my head. If I were convicted of another alcohol-related criminal offense while still under the court's supervision, that sentence would come crashing down on me and I would go to jail for all of the eighty days. It would likely end my new marriage and my career, and it would seriously jeopardize all relationships with family and friends. It would be a complete and total disaster, and my life, as I had known it, would effectively be over.

"Oh, shit," I said to myself, as a cold sweat broke out on my forehead. "Shit, shit, shit."

I stood up and walked back over to the windows, peering at the officers on the other side, some of whom were talking good naturedly to each other. I tentatively tapped on the glass to try to gently get their attention.

One of them looked at me and paused, seeming to take a second to decide if I was worth the effort of standing up and walking over. After a moment, he moved to the door and opened a slot.

"Yeah?" he said.

"Can you tell me what I'm charged with, and if I'm going to be released?" I asked as politely as I could.

"Name?"

"Timothy Michael Murtaugh," I said.

"Hang on," he said, and went back to a desk for a moment. When he returned, he had an answer.

"You gotta sober up and then we'll process you out," he said. "You have to get under the legal limit. Might be a few hours. We'll test you after a while."

"And what am I charged with?" I asked.

"Public intoxication."

"Okay," I said, and then had a thought about my personal possessions. "Do you guys have my wallet and phone and stuff?"

"It would have been taken from you and placed in a bag until you're released," he explained.

"Right, but I'm wondering about one thing. I had a coin, about the size of a silver dollar," I said. "It's a commemorative coin that has my grandfather's face on it. I had it in my left back pocket and it's gone. I wanted to make sure you have it and that I didn't lose it somewhere else."

He didn't answer, so I continued.

"It's my good luck charm," I said. We made eye contact through the window as I looked at him with what I imagined was a pathetic expression.

"It didn't work," he said.

1

Blackout Drunk
High School and College

The first time I got blackout drunk was at my buddy Mike Fisher's house, either sophomore or junior year of high school. Mike, with whom I'm still close friends today, lived just a few blocks away from my house in our small suburban Philadelphia town of Folsom, within Ridley Township in Delaware County, Pennsylvania. It was a mostly blue-collar town and a perfectly fine place to grow up.

I lived with my parents, Tim and Janet Murtaugh, and my brother Steve, who was six years younger. My mother's parents, Harry and Alice Cotton, lived in the same neighborhood as we did, and my dad's mother Kathleen lived in the neighboring community of Woodlyn. My paternal grandfather, Danny Murtaugh, had died in 1976, but had been a local celebrity as the successful manager of the Pittsburgh Pirates in Major League Baseball, and a two-time winner of the World Series. His name was still very well known locally, even many years later, and it was his face on a coin, a collectible produced by the Pirates, that I carried with me as a good luck piece.

My father retired as an Allstate insurance agent, but he had spent his younger years chasing his own baseball dreams as a catcher and then as a manager in the Pirates system. My mother had been a nurse, and then worked with my dad at the insurance office. I was not keenly aware of it at all times, but my father was an active alcoholic for years, until he stopped drinking when I was a freshman in college.

But while I was in high school one weekend, Mike's mother was away (his father had died while we were in elementary school), which meant there was an available house for a party, of sorts. A group of guys got together at his place and raided the bar, though Mike himself didn't drink. Someone made a large cocktail in a pint glass that had a lot of different things dumped into it, including green crème de menthe, and one of the guys dubbed it the "Christmas Tree." There was another offensive concoction that someone else called a "Flying Fuck at the Moon." Nasty as they were, I guess I drank quite enough of them, and probably a bunch of other stuff, because I got really intoxicated and don't remember much of the evening.

Naturally, I had told my parents that I was staying over at Mike's, neglecting to mention that his mother wasn't home. All of us slept on the floor with sleeping bags, and I woke up to a tremendous hangover.

As I waded through the fog in my brain, I tried to put together some pieces of memory, but was having a hard time making anything coherent out of it. I did recall that some of the guys had subjected me to a kind of interview the night before. I remember being asked questions about some of our classmates at school, as the guys tried to draw out my opinions of various people. More concerned with feeling physically terrible, and how I would describe the previous evening to my parents, I didn't think much about this "interview" at the time.

On Monday, I had recovered, and the hangover was mostly forgotten by the time I got to school. But that's when the antics of Friday night came back on me with vengeance, and I experienced an alcoholic's embarrassment and remorse for the first time.

Unbeknownst to me, while I was seriously inebriated, Mike and the other guys had produced a cassette tape recorder (remember, this was the mid- to late 1980s) and had documented my answers to their questions. The commentary was not something I wanted my classmates to hear, but Mike had brought it to school.

Of course, I was pretty pissed at Mike and the rest of the guys for humiliating me that way, but now, with the benefit of years of experience with embarrassing situations caused by my alcohol consumption, I know that I gave them the ammunition. If I hadn't gotten completely shitfaced and overridden my verbal filter, there would have been no embarrassing tape.

Perversely, it occurs to me now that I should have been grateful for what I perceived back then as a shocking betrayal by friends. They were showing me that nothing good comes from getting blind drunk, and a person other than me might have used the incident as a motivator to stay away from alcoholic binges in the future. But all I did was to vow that the next time I got hammered around my buddies, I'd be more careful about what I said, and I'd always be on the lookout for tape recorders.

By the time I graduated from Ridley Senior High School in June 1987 and headed to college at the end of the summer, I was really getting good at drinking. I started at Syracuse University, where I had been admitted to the prestigious S.I. Newhouse School of Public Communications.

Even though I was a broadcast journalism major, enrolled in a first-tier journalism school, I wanted to leave right away. The weather was God-awful and depressing, I got along terribly with one of my roommates, and I missed my friends from high school, many of whom were in colleges or universities close to our hometown.

So, just a few weeks into my first semester of college, I told my parents that I wanted to transfer, and we settled on Temple University in Philadelphia. It was obviously closer to home, had weather I was used to, and had a journalism program that was also nationally recognized, if not as world-renowned as the one at Syracuse.

I was getting good grades in what I knew would be my only semester at Syracuse, but that didn't stop me from cutting loose quite a bit. It was then that I think I began to subconsciously separate people into two camps defined by whether they regularly drank alcohol or not. If you take it a step further, I think I also divided the drinking camp into two tiers: those who drank somewhat normally, and those who drank like me. It's not hard to guess which people I hung around with the most.

Interestingly, while I was spending my short time in Syracuse, my father entered an alcohol rehabilitation facility to address his own drinking problems, which again I must confess I did not realize were that bad. This was in the fall of 1987, and as far as I know, he never took another drink again. If there was a lesson to be learned for me in his experiences, it was lost on me at the time, because I did nothing to alter my own path toward the same kinds of issues.

When I got to Temple, I was already into a drinking routine that had long before spilled outside of just weekends, where it had once been contained. Some of the guys in my dorm routinely drank from 40-ounce bottles of malt liquor because they were readily available from the convenience stores near the North Philadelphia campus, even to underage students.

I can still remember some of the brands. There was Olde English 800, King Cobra, St. Ides, and of course, Colt 45. Some guys claimed to prefer one from Schlitz they called "The Bull," which came in a brown bottle wrapped in a silver label with a blue bull on it. At first, I didn't like the taste of malt liquor all that much, but when I discovered that it contained more alcohol than regular beer, I became a convert.

Every year at Temple there was an event called Spring Fling, which was basically an outdoor music and drinking festival. Only a small percentage of students lived on campus, but for us it was fantastic to have a giant party right outside our dorm room door. This was where I first heard the phrase, "You can't drink all day if you don't start in the morning."

And we were very clever about availing ourselves of the best drinking opportunities we could find. One was in a bar that we frequented in Center City Philadelphia called, incongruously, the Beverly Hills Bar & Grill. It had an amazing deal on Thursday nights at the time—seven dollars to get in, with an open bar from 8 p.m. until closing at 2 a.m.

The bar was located right by Independence Hall, where the Founding Fathers had signed the Declaration of Independence in 1776; it was also within sight of the Liberty Bell. As experts in the field, my friends and I all knew that the key to getting a group of underaged dudes into a bar with moderately strict age verification was to have at least two good fake IDs at your disposal. Three good fakes were even better, or if there was someone in the posse who was already really twenty-one years old, that would work as well.

The scheme was simple, but it took a little bit of courage the first few times you tried it. Here's how it went: If you had three total IDs, then three guys would go in together in the first wave of the operation. Assuming that all three made it in safely, they would stay inside for a few minutes before just one of them went back outside with all three driver's licenses in his pocket, being sure on his way out to get his hand stamped if it was required for re-entry.

The IDs would then be delivered to the guys who were still waiting outside, and they would attempt to get past the bouncers themselves, being careful to wait a little while and go in separately. The initial guy with the hand stamp—the courier—could go back inside any time he wanted. This process would be repeated as many times as was required to secure everyone's entry into the bar.

We referred to this technique as "the *Hogan's Heroes* routine," after the late 1960s and early 1970s television sitcom that we had watched in re-run syndication for many years, and which featured the antics of a group of Allied servicemen being held in a German World War II prisoner of war camp. In many episodes, the good guys were able to fool their gullible captors through simple tricks, like passing a stolen code book from man to man down a formation, so that no one was caught with the book while he was being searched by the guards. Maybe it wasn't exactly applicable to what we were doing, but that's what we called it anyway.

The all-you-can-drink-for-seven-dollars deal was so good I got my friends from home to hit it with me over the summer. One night at closing time, a group of us—three guys and two girls—spilled out of the bar and drunkenly took in a couple of the historic sites in the neighborhood.

We laughed about the idea that a drunk person walking past Independence Hall could pull out a hundred-dollar bill, turn it over, and see a picture of the same building on the back of the money and do a double take at the real thing. Some of us actually rolled around on the ground because we wanted to "roll in the historic grass" near Independence Hall and the Liberty Bell.

While we were doing this, a couple of guys approached us, asking for a ride across one of the bridges over the Delaware River to New Jersey. They were belligerent, and we were feeling pretty sure of ourselves as well. Sensing that there was about to be a fight, one of my buddies bent down to make sure that his casual Adidas Samba soccer sneakers were tied. As he did that, I faced one of the two bad guys, stupidly placed my right hand on his left shoulder, and said condescendingly, "Now, listen here, son—"

I never even saw his unimpeded right hand coming up to punch me in the mouth, so it was jarring and entirely unexpected. His fist connected and I went down in a hurry, rolling on the historic ground once more as a result. The other villain simultaneously coldcocked the third high school pal, meaning two of us were on the deck in the blink of an eye. The girls started screaming.

The timing of all this was such that at this exact moment, the last one of us was straightening up from checking his shoelaces, and found himself facing both enemy combatants. They knocked him down as well, with one of them kicking him in the face badly enough that it chipped a tooth. The two guys ran away, and that was the end of the fight.

We licked our wounds and took stock of our injuries at the twenty-four-hour Denny's restaurant in Tinicum near the Philadelphia airport. I had a fat lip that I could conceal by tightening my mouth and forcing the swelling down, and my buddy had a chipped tooth, which he had to address by going to the dentist the next day.

I don't believe my parents ever found out about what happened that night, but I did learn a couple of important lessons. First, if you're drunk, don't do stupid things to guarantee that someone is going to punch you. Second, always remember that even if you don't want to fight, sometimes the other guy does.

Hearing this story, it may surprise some people that "try not to drink so much" was not on the list of lessons I learned that night, but truthfully, the thought never crossed my mind.

I want to say that I drank consistently throughout college and that it wasn't any more than my friends did, but that wouldn't be true. I drank more than anyone I knew, it was increasing, and it was punctuated with occasional episodes that were more embarrassing or alarming than just a regular one-too-many outing. These weren't things that I could see at the time, of course, but they are obvious to me now, decades later.

I got a student job in the athletic department as a statistician and spotter for the professional play-by-play broadcasters for Temple basketball and football games. It was a fantastic gig for a kid who was a sports fan, as it gave me the incredible opportunity to work both home and away games, including getting a regular seat on the team charter flights for road football games. The job also required me to sit between the two announcers during games, keeping track of stats and any trends, jotting down notes, or pointing to the names of players and using hand signals to give cues for describing the game action.

It was about this time that I realized that I am one of those people who really reeks of alcohol on the mornings after big drunks. My physical proximity to the announcers allowed them to detect the alcoholic fumes coming off me.

During a commercial break on one Saturday afternoon basketball game, play-by-play man Don Henderson, a veteran Philadelphia sportscaster who enjoyed a long career, said to me, "Out late last night, Timmy?"

"Not really, why?" I said, trying to sound innocent.

"You smell like a Smirnoff truck ran over you," he said, referencing one of the best-selling brands of vodka. I didn't reply and just concentrated on getting everything right for the rest of the game, to demonstrate that whatever he suspected, it was not interfering with my ability to do my job.

It was probably the first time that anyone had ever called out my drinking in a professional environment. And though I was embarrassed, I'm quite sure that I didn't take the remark to heart, and it certainly didn't influence my behavior for the better.

Another time one fall, when I lived in an apartment at the corner of N. 15th Street and Green Street in Philadelphia with a few other Temple students, I awoke on Friday morning to the loud sounds of conversation and laughing outside on the street. My bedroom was in the basement level of a two-floor apartment in a town house, and the window was at sidewalk level. Benjamin Franklin High School was right nearby and the voices I heard were likely from a group of students.

My head was pounding and my mouth was dry, and all I knew in the moment was that I was furious to have been awakened in such a manner. I had been drinking hard the night before and was in no mood for people in good spirits, so I got out of bed, made a fist, and rapped on the window sharply with the knuckles of my right hand.

The glass shattered and the kids outside reacted with a "Whoa!" and then laughter as they quickly realized what had happened. They moved off a little ways, leaving me inside the bedroom to contemplate what to do next.

My window was broken and a glance at my right hand showed that I was bleeding, and not just a little bit. I stood there pondering next steps as the cool, fall, outdoor air entered my bedroom through the broken window. I looked at the clock and saw that I was due at the airport in about an hour to catch the charter for a Temple football trip.

Few college students have looked as motivated and pathetic as I must have appeared as I scrambled for something to use as a patch for the window. I remember I found an empty cardboard case for a Miller Lite twenty-four-pack and cut a panel out of it to place over the gaping hole in the glass, taping it in place with clear packing tape. I wrapped some paper towels around my bloody hand and used the same tape to hold it in place as tightly as possible until the bleeding stopped.

I showered and got dressed and packed a bag as fast as humanly possible, pausing on my way out the door only to shotgun two beers from the refrigerator, back-to-back at the kitchen sink, to begin to push the hangover away a little bit. Hauling ass out to N. Broad Street just a block away, I desperately hailed a cab and raced to the airport to catch the plane.

By some miracle, I made it before takeoff and walked down the center aisle on the plane as calmly as possible, looking for a seat where I wouldn't have to sit next to anyone. By then the bleeding had mostly stopped and I had my cut hand, wrapped in a fresh paper towel, hidden in my jacket pocket.

Henderson, the announcer, boomed out in his deep voice for all to hear, "Cutting it a little close, aren't we Timmy?"

As I found a seat, I checked the cut on my hand and confirmed that it wasn't too bad. I would just put a large Band-Aid on it later and it would be fine. As we taxied out for takeoff minutes later, I did take one lesson away from this sorry episode: next time, set an alarm.

I don't recall any self-promises of drinking less.

2

Capitol Hill to the Trump Administration
2016 to 2017

I was sober for the final twenty months, out of four years, that I was communications director for Congressman Lou Barletta.

Barletta, from northeastern Pennsylvania, was dying to endorse Donald Trump as the Republican presidential primaries were unfolding in early 2016. He had been very enthusiastic about Trump's candidacy since that first golden escalator ride in New York City, because when Trump talked about eliminating illegal immigration, he was speaking Barletta's language.

"This is the first guy who has ever said the same things that I say about illegal immigration," Barletta said to us about Trump. "The way he describes the problem is exactly what we've experienced in Hazleton."

And when he ultimately endorsed Trump, that's the main reason he gave.

"Donald Trump was criticized the same way I was criticized when I was mayor, because he addressed an important issue," he told *Politico*.

"I don't believe the issue would have been addressed if it wasn't for Donald Trump bringing it up."

Truth be told, other Barletta staffers and I had tried to talk him out of endorsing Trump because we didn't believe that he would win the nomination, but Barletta was insistent. When he announced his support in mid-March 2016, he was the third House member to do so, and he was annoyed with us that we'd delayed him long enough to keep him from being first.

Once Barletta had endorsed, the whole office was all in on Trump, and I frequently accompanied the congressman to the presidential campaign surrogate meetings across the street at the Capitol Hill Club. It's where I nabbed my first red MAGA hat—Make America Great Again—that would become the enduring symbol of that campaign. At one of those meetings, I spotted Justin Clark across the room. He'd been the political director on Linda McMahon's Senate campaign in Connecticut in 2012, where I had briefly been campaign comms director (more on that later), and had recently been named Trump's deputy national political director.

I followed the 2016 presidential election through Barletta's eyes, including when he stuck by Trump while others wavered or bolted, in the wake of the infamous *Access Hollywood* tape. And I watched the culmination of that campaign at home on my couch on election night, feeding a bottle to my first child, a son who'd been born just eight days before.

Our son had been born on Halloween 2016, and his arrival turned everything in our house upside down, something to which other first-time parents can probably relate. We were just beginning the exhausting months of multiple overnight feedings as Election Day approached, so the little guy and I spent a lot of time together watching cable news shows when it was my turn with the baby bottle. On television, everyone anticipated the election of Hillary Clinton as president.

But as we watched, on November 8, 2016, something unexpected happened. Donald J. Trump was elected president of the United States, marking a big inflection point for the country, which was about to pivot away from Barack Obama's presidency and toward a self-described America First administration. And it marked a major turning point in my own life, although I didn't know it at the time.

A little more than two months later, on January 19, 2017—the day before Inauguration Day—news broke that President-elect Trump had selected Sonny Perdue, the former governor of Georgia, to be his secretary of agriculture. I had never met Governor Perdue, nor had I ever worked for him. But I knew people who had.

I sent a text to Nick Ayers, my old boss at the Republican Governors Association (again, more on that later), who had been one of Governor Perdue's top aides for years. I didn't get a response from Nick, but not long after the inauguration, I did receive a phone call inviting me to a screening interview, which of course I gladly accepted.

A few days after that initial meeting, I had a meeting with Perdue himself, in which I sheepishly disclosed that I had a terribly checkered alcoholic past, complete with arrests and convictions for DUI and other alcohol-related charges. He didn't seem bothered by that.

"Are you drinking today?" he asked.

I said I wasn't, and he nodded his head as if to indicate that the answer was fine with him. Some weeks later, I turned in my notice to Representative Barletta—not an easy thing to do since he had meant an awful lot to me—and joined the Trump administration in the U.S. Department of Agriculture, though Perdue himself would not be confirmed by the Senate until almost the end of April.

On Perdue's first full day as a member of the Trump Cabinet on April 25, 2017, I barely knew him, even though I was his communications director at the Department of Agriculture. There was a busy day planned, and right out of the gate it was "local media day" over at the White House campus, with all cabinet secretaries expected to attend.

At the Eisenhower Executive Office Building, right across from the West Wing on the White House grounds, radio and television stations from around the country had assembled. White House communications staff paraded cabinet members and other high-level administration officials through the large and ornate Indian Treaty Room for quick interviews, one after another.

Perdue made quick work of the interviews, and I found his security detail and walked with our whole group out of the room, accompanied now by a man named Ray Starling, who was President Trump's top advisor on agricultural issues. Once in the hallway, the group turned a different way than I had expected, and, hustling to catch up, I asked where we were going.

"We're going across the street to talk to the boss," Perdue said to me over his shoulder.

"What boss?" I asked, although I thought I knew the answer.

"I've only got one boss," he said.

At that point, early in the spring of 2017, I had never met President Trump.

"What are we talking to him about?" I asked.

"We're going to try to save NAFTA," Perdue said without elaboration.

For the previous few weeks, official Washington had been abuzz with the speculation that Trump, who had been relentlessly critical of the North American Free Trade Agreement (NAFTA), was about to announce that the US was abruptly withdrawing from the treaty. News could come at any time that the US was walking away from its partners in the deal, Canada and Mexico, and many feared that chaos would erupt in world markets if the agreement were simply abandoned rather than renegotiated.

Starling led the way as we took the steep exterior steps down to cross West Executive Avenue and entered the West Wing. I knew I didn't have the right kind of visitor's badge around my neck, so I tried to stay with our team as we wound our way through the tight hallways. Starling was briefing the secretary about the plan—whatever it was—as we walked.

The next thing I knew, we were standing outside the Oval Office. I knew that because the door to the famous room was open and I could hear Trump's voice coming from within. Starling was speaking to Madeleine Westerhout, who was Trump's gatekeeper outside. We were asked to wait in the Cabinet Room, which was just off the space we were in, opposite "The Oval," as it is known in shorthand.

Perdue, Starling, and I went into the Cabinet Room, accompanied by Perdue's security detail, which included Matt Sloan, a good guy who had protected the previous secretary of agriculture as well and who would become a friend. We sat cooling our heels, and I nervously wondered what in the world was in store for us.

A quiet conversation about strategy between Perdue and Starling was interrupted when the door flew open and Reince Priebus, Trump's first chief of staff, burst in. He walked quickly to stand in front of Perdue, looking rushed and unhappy.

"Who just shows up at the Oval Office without an appointment?" Priebus asked rhetorically. "Who just drops in?"

He pulled a rectangular card out of his pocket, and I could see the White House stationery markings at the top. There was a lot of text on it, and he held it up to show Perdue as a visual aid for the point he was making.

"See this?" he asked. "This is today's schedule. We are about here." He pointed at the text in a spot which approximated the current time of day, which was midmorning.

SWING HARD IN CASE YOU HIT IT

"If you show up at the Oval Office without an appointment, it screws up everything down here," he said, sliding his finger up and down along lower part of the card, which presumably showed the president's schedule for that afternoon and evening. "We'll get hopelessly behind, and we'll never be able to catch up."

He took a breather and waited to see if we had any excuse for our rudeness in being present.

"Can you understand that?" Priebus prompted.

Perdue looked at him with a blank expression, and said in an innocent voice, "It's my first day."

I had to bite my lip to stop a hard laugh from coming out, and I could see that Perdue's poker face was impressive. Priebus wasn't amused, though.

"You want to talk about NAFTA?" Priebus asked. "You're almost too late. That train is leaving the station."

"I just want to talk to the president about what it would mean for farmers, because they're his people," Perdue said. "They helped put him in that office over there and I think he should know what they think about it."

Priebus thought about that for a moment. "Wait here," he said, and left.

Perdue looked around at our little posse and shrugged. "I didn't think there was time to go through their process," he explained.

As a two-term former governor, longtime state legislator, and successful agri-businessman, Sonny Perdue was not accustomed to being lectured by anyone, I'm sure. So, it was impressive to watch him calmly absorb Priebus's scolding without reacting, because what he really wanted was to get into the Oval Office to talk Trump out of withdrawing from NAFTA without a new trade deal in place. And if that meant taking a tongue lashing from the White House chief of staff, then that's what he would do.

This was my first experience with Secretary Perdue, and it was rapidly clear that he was an impressive guy to be around, and I would come to learn that he was highly demanding and extremely fair, and exhibited an amazingly even personality. He had a quick wit, a good sense of humor, and was always polite. I've heard it said about some people in positions of authority, but it was certainly true in Perdue's case: he could get angry from time to time, but the last thing you wanted to do was disappoint him, because that was the worst thing of all. I would thoroughly enjoy working for him, and today I retain the highest respect for him as a person and a leader.

Finally, someone came to the door with the news that the president would see us, and we walked briskly out of the Cabinet Room, across the outer office, and then through the door of the most storied office in the world. The Oval Office was just like it looks on television and in pictures, although it wasn't as big as I thought it would be.

The president was seated behind the Resolute Desk, with chairs aligned in front of him, which Perdue and Starling went to occupy. Trump's trade advisor, Peter Navarro, was also present. As soon as I entered the room, I slid to the left, against the wall near a bust of Abraham Lincoln off to the president's right. I stood still and tried not to make any movements that would draw attention to myself.

Perdue began by telling the president that he hoped that the administration would not announce a sudden withdrawal from NAFTA, as stories in the media indicated was about to happen, because it would create great tumult in agricultural circles.

"NAFTA isn't perfect, Mr. President, but by and large, our farmers have done fairly well under the deal," Perdue said. "If it just went away without anything to replace it, it would cause a lot of harm. They're in a panic right now about what might happen. For some agricultural products, NAFTA could use some work, but for most it's actually been pretty good."

Trump showed mild surprise at the news that there were some Americans who actually liked NAFTA, and he turned to Starling for confirmation. Ray reiterated what Perdue had said and allowed that farmers saw the trade deal differently than, say, workers in manufacturing, where NAFTA had been indisputably bad for business. Trump took that in for a second, and then seemed to notice me to his right for the first time.

"Who's this?" he asked Perdue, pointing in my direction.

"That's Tim Murtaugh," Perdue said. "He does our communications at USDA."

As my heart leapt up into my throat, I nodded a greeting to the president without speaking, and he returned his attention to the people sitting in front of his desk. After a minute or two more of discussion, he suddenly turned his head to face me again.

"Tim, what do you think about this?" President Trump asked, startling me by remembering my name.

I paused for a second, as I had not expected to have a speaking role in the meeting, and then just rephrased what I had heard both Perdue and Starling explain.

"We all know that most Americans think NAFTA was a bad deal, as you've pointed out," I think I said. "But if you ask farmers, most of them will tell you that they actually like NAFTA and that it's been good for them, on balance."

Trump took that in for a beat, and then turned back to Perdue and Starling to see if they had anything to add. By then, Jared Kushner, his advisor and son-in-law, had entered the room and was also involved in the conversation. It's my recollection that he was viewing the agricultural arguments against withdrawing from NAFTA abruptly as persuasive, while Navarro was unmistakably against anything that would prevent the immediate removal of the US from the trade deal.

Perdue reached into his suit coat pocket and pulled out some papers, unfolding them and placing them on the desk in front of the president. From my vantage point, I could see that they appeared to be color-coded maps of the United States, and whatever they represented, I hadn't seen them before.

"I'd like to show you something, Mr. President," Perdue said, situating the two little maps on the desk in front of Trump.

He pointed to the map closest to Trump's right hand. "This is a map of the 2016 election. The red is for counties that you won, and the blue is the counties that Hillary Clinton won. You can see the big swath of red right through the whole middle of the country."

Perdue then drew the president's attention to the map by his left hand. "And this one shows the counties that will be the hardest hit if NAFTA disappears, based on what crops are grown there. The red areas are the ones that will really be crushed."

Perdue pushed the two maps together, so they were side by side in front of the president.

"The maps are the same, Mr. President," Perdue said. "These are your people. They're the ones who'll get hurt if you withdraw from NAFTA and don't have something to replace it with."

Trump looked at Perdue, looked down at the maps again, and nodded his head. Kushner abruptly thanked everyone, and the meeting ended. We walked out, and just like that, my first visit to the Oval Office was over. Total duration: probably less than ten minutes.

We still weren't headed out of the building, however, because Starling led us to a different room where he and the secretary were evidently going to take part in another meeting. That was the Roosevelt Room, a frequently used, medium-sized space with a long table, that was named after the two presidents with that surname. Used for many purposes over the years, the room was also the scene where Bill

Clinton uttered his famous line, "I did not have sexual relations with that woman, Miss Lewinsky."

On that day in 2017, however, it was the setting for a meeting to plan the step-by-step removal of the United States from the trilateral trade deal with Canada and Mexico, should the president order it so. The timeline began with a letter from the White House to Congress to announce the intent to withdraw. It was clear to me, just from the very fact that this meeting had been scheduled and was taking place, that the sudden withdrawal from NAFTA was real and imminent.

After just a few minutes, one of the doors to the Roosevelt Room opened and Kushner stuck his head in.

"Is this the NAFTA withdrawal meeting?" he asked.

Several staffers nodded their heads to confirm that it was.

"Okay," Kushner said, waving his hand like he was wiping something away. "This isn't happening. The withdrawal isn't happening. You can break it up."

He closed the door and disappeared again.

Word began to spread quickly, and soon was reported openly in the press, that Trump had elected to call for a renegotiation of NAFTA, rather than pull out of the existing deal with nothing to fall back on. Some articles and subsequent books by journalists about the administration included some of the details of what Secretary Perdue had done that day, but nothing was like experiencing it in person.

We were very careful at the Department of Agriculture about publicly giving the secretary too much credit for calming fears about a sudden end to an important trade deal because it was the president's decision, after all, and he was the boss. Indeed, I heard Perdue say many times that even on occasions when it appeared that Trump had made up his mind, he still usually left a little door open in his brain to consider alternatives.

3

The Road Leads to Virginia
1991 to 1993

As I was getting ready to graduate from Temple in December 1991, it was time to think about finding a job, and I had decided that I wanted to be a baseball play-by-play announcer. My father said he'd pay for me to travel to the baseball winter meetings, which that year were being held in Miami in December.

I flew south for a few days with a stack of résumés and a bunch of audition tapes filled with my basketball and football radio play-by-play highlights and a half inning of baseball I'd recorded by myself while sitting in the last row of the upper deck at a Phillies game. I actually had done a lot of play-by-play—for the Temple women's basketball team, for a minor league professional men's basketball team in Philadelphia, and for area high school football games.

The baseball winter meetings are an annual gathering of Major League Baseball executives, scouts, and media—always somewhere warm—where they discuss possible rules changes, make trades, and do other kinds of business that surrounds a professional sport.

There were also usually a lot of job seekers in attendance, and I was one of them.

The headquarters for the meetings was the ritzy Fontainebleau Hotel in Miami Beach. That's not where I was staying, mind you, but that's where I spent a lot of time. There were large meeting spaces set aside for people looking for baseball jobs, including in broadcasting, and there were postings for available positions. I remember that for the minor league radio jobs, which were where I was aiming, you actually put your résumés and tapes in manila envelopes and placed them into what looked like empty plastic U.S. Mail bins, each labeled with the team that was doing the hiring.

My father had set up a breakfast meeting for me on one of the days with an important minor league executive with a very famous name. Except for that, there wasn't much structure around my plans. I was in Miami Beach for a few days without much to do, so naturally I drank as much as I could.

I woke up with a dry mouth and pounding headache the morning of my breakfast meeting, feeling a little hazy and probably a little drunk still. It took me a second to realize where I was, and I looked at the time; it was after 7:30 a.m. I had been out drinking at South Beach until pretty late.

"SHIT!" I yelled, flinging the bed covers off and jumping to my feet. I began to frantically scramble around for a clean set of clothes in my duffel bag, calculating how likely it would be that I would make it to the Fontainebleau by 8 a.m. Because these were the days before cell phones, I didn't know of a way to alert anyone that I'd probably be late.

When I got to the hotel twenty minutes late, I quick-walked to the restaurant, where I scanned the place for customers sitting alone at their tables, although I didn't really know the man I was looking for.

I found a likely suspect and made my way to his table. He stood as I approached, so my guess had proved to be accurate.

We shook hands and introduced ourselves to each other. He was a man in his mid-forties, wearing a suit and looking prosperous. I was twenty-two, wearing God-only-knows-what, and hungover as hell.

"I'm sorry I'm late," I managed.

"That's fine," he said. "Now, tell me what you're interested in doing in baseball."

His name was Branch Rickey III, and he was the new president of the American Association, one of the minor leagues at the Triple-A level, one rung below the big leagues. I was hoping he could help me, that is, if he decided to give me any advice after I had nearly stood him up and arrived late, looking like I had just rolled out of bed after a long bender. Because I had.

He was well known in baseball circles for being a scout and executive in the Pittsburgh Pirates and Cincinnati Reds organization before he became president of the American Association earlier in that year of 1991. And he was also known as the grandson of the legendary Major League Baseball executive Branch Rickey, who, as president and general manager of the Brooklyn Dodgers, signed Jackie Robinson to break baseball's color barrier in 1947.

I can't remember our conversation verbatim, but I know that this was one of those occasions where I was swinging hard in case I hit it, because Rickey was a big-time contact for someone like me. I told him about my experience in sports broadcasting to that point, which was quite a lot for a twenty-two-year-old, I thought. He asked about my father, who had helped to set up the meeting, and he gave me some tips about the interviews I hoped I would soon be having with minor league teams from lower levels.

Looking back on the conversation now, I have no doubt that I was an embarrassing mess. I must have reeked of alcohol, my eyes were probably bloodshot and glassy, and there's a pretty good chance that my hands were shaking. I don't see how it was possible that I left a good impression.

Our chat was brief, certainly less than thirty minutes, which I think was plenty long enough for him to spend with a kid who had been inconsiderately late, and who had obviously been out drinking the night before. He was generous with his time and advice, and I thanked him for it before I excused myself so he could continue his morning. It would be many years before we spoke again.

The twenty-two-year-old version of myself walked away from that table having taken the wrong lesson away from the entire incident. Instead of being appalled at my own behavior—drinking to excess the night before an early meeting, and then being late to the appointment—I was actually feeling good. Sure, I had nearly missed it completely, but it had turned out okay, right?

I didn't yet comprehend what it meant to earn a reputation as a problematic drinker. But that would come.

In the end, my trip to the baseball winter meetings resulted in just one sit-down interview with a team—a Class A level ballclub from Bend, Oregon, called the Bucks, who were about to become affiliated with the new Colorado Rockies. It was a low minor league, short season situation, but it was a foot in the door, and I desperately wanted the job.

I became a finalist, but it was not to be. The other candidate, whoever he was, got the job instead, and I went back to Philadelphia empty-handed. I do remember being hungover again during the interview, but I can't say that it caused me to miss out on the job. I can't, however, imagine that it helped.

Rather than sticking it out and continuing to pursue a baseball radio job, I accepted the only offer I already had in hand and prepared to move to Spotsylvania County, Virginia, near the historic town of Fredericksburg, in early 1992.

I spent two years there, at radio station B101.5 FM, WBQB, and its sister AM station WFVA, anchoring the evening drive-time newscasts. I also covered stories of local interest, including Fredericksburg City Council meetings and an occasional Spotsylvania County Board of Supervisors meeting.

It was a decent first job in broadcasting, and the guy who hired me, news director John Calhoun, was a genuinely nice older man who really seemed to care about his younger employees. They paid me the princely sum of $22,000 a year, which seemed about right for first news jobs as far as I could tell, and I felt like I was the king of the world. I was getting paid as a full-time radio journalist, I learned that being an on-air personality in a small town was kind of cool, and I was supporting myself out in the real world.

My schedule was mostly a breeze: I worked Monday through Friday from noon to 6 p.m., recording short newscasts for the AM station and preparing for two five-minute casts at 5 p.m. and 6 p.m. The one downside was that every other week I had to anchor newscasts on Saturday morning starting at 7 a.m.

Overall, it was a pretty great schedule for a committed drinker. Getting off the air at 6 p.m. meant that I could make it to happy hour, stay in bed the next morning until 11:30, and still make it to work on time. The occasional Saturday morning shift was a serious drag, and barely survivable. I guarantee that I performed each early-morning newscast while partially drunk, tending toward hungover, reeking of booze, and craving my next drink.

As time went by, I passed the two-year mark at the radio station and became somewhat panicked that I would get stuck working at the same place for my entire career. I began to move then, toward the obvious next step on the path: local television news instead of radio.

4

Growing Family, Advancing Career
USDA, 2018

My job as communications director for the U.S. Department of Agriculture (USDA) required a Top Secret security clearance, which someone told me was necessary because I had access to information that could potentially move commodities markets. It was not clear to me, however, whether I would pass the background check that went along with the clearance, and there was the risk that I would lose the job if I failed.

I filled out a long questionnaire, which probed around to judge what kind of threat I posed to the existence of the United States, and whether I had personal habits that could make me susceptible to blackmail attempts. After that, there was an in-person interview, and then investigators had similar conversations with some selected family and friends.

Of course, I was completely truthful in my answers, though it seemed odd to me that I was already in my position as comms director before the clearance had been granted. I learned that this was often the way the federal government worked.

I told the investigators about my past, including my arrests (which they would find anyway) and my history of alcoholism, the full details of which they may not have known if I hadn't told them. I also answered honestly about casual drug use years before—marijuana and a little cocaine—and submitted a sample for a urine test. It was a very disconcerting experience to admit all these things to representatives of law enforcement who held my career in their hands, but I had been told that they mainly cared that I was being honest.

After my participation in the background check was over, I held my breath while the interviews with friends and family were conducted.

The interaction that my wife Dena experienced did not fill me with confidence. After some preliminary questions meant to establish her own identity and occupation, the topic of conversation turned to me.

"And why am I talking to you today?" the investigator asked. "How do you know Timothy Murtaugh?"

Dena paused for a second before answering, "Uh, he's my husband."

"Yes, of course," was the reply, accompanied by shuffling of paper because Dena had just supplied what was apparently unexpected information. "I'm sure that's noted in here somewhere."

Despite my concerns about my history, and the somewhat un-nerving questions from the interviewers, I ultimately did receive my Top Secret clearance. It came, however, with a letter of warning to me that if I returned to erratic, alcohol-induced behavior, the decision could be revisited.

In the months that followed, Ray Starling would leave the White House and come over to USDA where he would become Sonny Perdue's chief of staff in May 2018, replacing Heidi Green. Heidi was a solid Perdue confidant from Georgia who was well liked by the political appointees at the department, but who had decided to return home to her family.

I got along famously with Heidi, and I sensed that I would like Ray as well. It was a common theme, I found, that the senior people with whom Sonny Perdue surrounded himself were well qualified, extremely professional, and a pleasure to work with.

One Friday in July 2018, I was at work early and getting in some exercise on an elliptical machine in the USDA gym. Dena called me from her cell phone and I answered while I was still working out. About six months pregnant with our second child, she was due in October, but said she was in distress and didn't feel right. She asked if I would pick her up and take her to the hospital.

I got dressed and rushed over to the Department of Homeland Security where she worked, also as a political appointee, and drove to Inova Fairfax, the Northern Virginia hospital where our first son had been born and where her doctor was. When we arrived, a quick examination showed that labor had already begun, and they administered some medicine to bring that to a stop.

"We're going to admit her and keep her in bed until this baby is born," the doctor said.

"For three months?" I asked, astonished.

"Uh, no, Mr. Murtaugh, it's not gonna be three months," the doctor said. "This baby is probably coming today."

We learned that because of an infection, the unborn baby basically hit the eject button and declared that it was time for him to come out. A little boy was born later that day by cesarean section at twenty-seven weeks of gestation, weighing in at two pounds, five ounces. He would spend the next seventy-seven days in the neonatal intensive care unit (NICU) at Inova Fairfax, meaning that the first eleven weeks of his life were spent in the hospital being fed the tiniest measurements of nutrients imaginable. Dena spent hour after hour with him in the NICU, every single day that he was a patient. As I write this, he is a normal, healthy, energetic five-year-old kindergartner who looks up to, but fights with, his big brother.

After the birth, I cut back on work-related travel, but I did still make the occasional trip. In October 2018, Secretary Perdue went to Indianapolis to speak to the annual convention of Future Farmers of America, which is a youth group that emphasizes leadership in agricultural learning. I might have skipped this one, if Ray Starling had not arranged for me to fly home from Indianapolis aboard Air Force One with Secretary Perdue. I didn't realize it at the time, but Ray had bumped himself off the manifest to make room for me to have my first flight on the president's plane, and he'd used up a favor with the White House to get it done.

At the time, I didn't know that I would be one day hold a senior position on the president's re-election campaign, so the chance to be in the president's bubble was extremely exciting. Riding to the airport as part of Trump's motorcade was incredible, as the highways were all completely closed off to other traffic. It's one thing to see it on television; it's another thing entirely to experience it.

Once aboard Air Force One, I had to locate my seat, which was marked with a little card with my name on it. I found myself seated next to John Pence, the vice president's nephew. He was also the son of Greg Pence, who would be elected to Congress in Indiana that coming November to fill the seat that his brother, the new VP, had occupied for twelve years. John Pence and I would later work together on the Trump 2020 re-election campaign, but I didn't know that at the time.

While we were in flight, I walked around to explore a little, though I was afraid of roaming too much because I didn't know what the rules were. I didn't see President Trump anywhere, but I found Secretary Perdue in a conference room having a casual conversation with some White House staffers, including Bill Stepien, Justin Clark, Stephen Miller, and Johnny DeStefano.

On our way home to Washington, DC, we were stopping in Murphysboro, Illinois, for a pre-midterm election rally, so I asked Secretary Perdue if he was planning to deplane for the event. He said that he wasn't going to the rally because he was afraid Trump would ask him to speak, and he didn't want to risk violating the Hatch Act by engaging in politics on government time. That made sense to me, but I told him that if he didn't mind, I was planning to attend. He said that was fine.

I climbed into another presidential motorcade that formed on the tarmac next to the airplane, for what would be a very short drive to a nearby hangar on the airport property, which was the location of the rally. This would be my very first Trump rally, and on that day, I couldn't know that I would eventually attend dozens of similar events over the course of the next two years.

Earlier, Trump had told the media that he considered canceling the rally in light of a mass shooting at the Tree of Life synagogue in Pittsburgh, where a gunman had killed eleven people and wounded six others during Shabbat services that morning. Trump said that he decided to proceed because he didn't want to show any deference to the accused killer, who had been taken into custody.

At the rally, Trump urged the crowd to unite against the ideas that drove the murderer to act.

"This evil anti-Semitic attack is an assault on all of us. It's an assault on humanity. It will require all of us working together to extract the hateful poison of anti-Semitism from the world," he said. "The scourge of anti-Semitism cannot be ignored, cannot be tolerated and cannot be allowed to continue."

He then launched into his standard rally address, ad-libbing quite a bit and launching bombs at his political adversaries. I spent the time roaming around backstage, ducking out into the crowd to check out that perspective, and trying to absorb every aspect of the event, because I didn't know if I'd ever be in that position again.

When it was over, it was back into the motorcade for the brief ride across the airport to Air Force One, where I found Secretary Perdue sitting in the conference room, engrossed in a University of Georgia football game on television. Perdue had been governor of Georgia, but he was also a University of Georgia graduate and had walked on to the football team as a quarterback his freshman year ("I was small but slow," he liked to joke, though he had been a major high school star who'd held several state passing records).

"This is why you didn't go to the rally?" I said, in a jokingly accusatory way. "The Hatch Act didn't have anything to do with it!"

"The Hatch Act is a powerful deterrent," Perdue said, and returned his attention to the game.

I had not told my parents about my ride aboard Air Force One in case it fell through, so I took the opportunity to call them from the plane. There was a phone inside the armrest of most seats, and mine put me in contact with an Air Force officer who asked for the number I was trying to reach and the name of the person I was calling.

When my parents answered the phone, the officer informed them that they had an incoming call from someone aboard Air Force One, and then they connected the lines. It was pretty awesome, though not unlike what happens when someone places a call from inside a jail or prison.

I spoke to my parents and also called Dena, and it occurred to me that it was a pretty amazing turnaround for a guy who had been a raging drunk only a short time before. In less than three and a half years, I'd gone from waking up in jail, almost certain that my life was over, to cruising on Air Force One at nearly 600 miles an hour.

5

Charlottesville and Richmond
1994 to 1996

I suspect that everyone can look back at decisions they've made and wonder how things would have turned out in the alternative. For me, I think of leaving Syracuse University and transferring to Temple—where would I have ended up if I had stayed? What if I had continued to pursue baseball jobs instead of moving to Virginia? I often wish it were possible to view the alternate timeline, the one that never had a chance to exist, because I had gone a different direction years before.

One of those course-changing events happened in early 1994 when I landed a job at WVIR-TV, the NBC affiliate in Charlottesville, Virginia. I started as a general assignment reporter from Wednesday through Friday, and then anchored the local news breaks during *The Today Show* on Saturday and Sunday mornings, while turning around stories for the evening news on those days as well.

Some interesting things happened, like the time Muhammad Ali, who I'd heard had a farm in nearby Nelson County, just showed up to hand out literacy pamphlets in the streets of a disadvantaged neighborhood in Charlottesville. Parkinson's disease already had ahold of the champ, and he didn't grant an interview. But I can say that I met him.

One day I was interviewing people in a local restaurant about the new phenomenon of indoor smoking bans, when I asked a few questions of a middle-aged dad with a couple of children. It wasn't until I got back to the station that someone saw my tape and identified that dad as Sam Shepard, actor and playwright, who lived with his longtime partner, actress Jessica Lange, somewhere outside of town. Come to think of it, he had looked a little familiar.

One Sunday morning, I burst into the control room with a stack of tapes for my first *Today Show* local news break of the day. It was just after 7 a.m. and I remember feeling clammy, still a little drunk, barely shaven, and bleary eyed.

I handed over a copy of my script and went into the studio, sat down on set, clipped the mic to my tie, and plugged in my earpiece cable. I had gotten into position with just a few seconds to spare, and as I awaited my cue, the director said into my ear that I had not left him enough time to sort through my tapes, load them into the machines, and cue them up for playing during my segment. He said that he would try to catch up, but that he couldn't promise anything.

With no choice but to press on, I launched into my script, got to the place where the first piece of tape should come in and—nothing happened.

"No tape," the director said in my ear, so I carried on with the written script in front of me. It went like that for the next three minutes, story after story with only script and no tape, before I finally threw it to commercial break.

There was a thirty-second ad, and I returned to give the weather forecast over some full-screen graphics that the weather people had prepared the night before.

SWING HARD IN CASE YOU HIT IT

"*The Today Show*, after this," I said, finishing the disastrous segment, and I put my head down on the desk.

"Goddammit," I said, failing to heed the old rule: always assume any microphone is hot.

Monday morning, which would normally have been the first of my two days off that week, I got a call that the news director wanted to see me. I made my way to the station and found his office.

"It's come to my attention that we had a 'Goddammit' go out over the air," he said. "What happened?"

I awkwardly tried to explain that I had lost track of time in the newsroom while preparing for the cut-in and blah-blah-blah. I got a one-day suspension, and I spent my extra day off castigating myself for allowing alcohol to interfere with my job...while getting drunk again. I returned to work hungover, having learned exactly nothing.

I had been in Charlottesville for less than a year when a former local Republican congressman, George Allen, became governor. The general manager of the station decided to open a full-time Richmond bureau and I volunteered. ("Let me get this straight, I get to live in Richmond, seventy miles away from any bosses? Count me in.")

Moving to Richmond introduced me to state-level politics and it helped me to create relationships with the people who were important in that arena. It also gave me sustained, up-close looks at grand government buildings for the first time.

The first significant event that I covered was a press conference in late summer of 1994, hosted by Governor Allen on the South Portico of the State Capitol building in Richmond. If you've never been to Richmond, it is well worth the time to take a tour of the magnificent seat of Virginia's government. Designed by Thomas Jefferson, the Capitol's cornerstone was laid in a ceremony in 1785 with Governor Patrick Henry in attendance. I came to love the Virginia State Capitol, to take pride in working there, and I showed it off to visitors any chance I got.

And, amazingly, my television job was just perfect for a heavy drinker. Funny how that worked out.

The Virginia legislature, the General Assembly, only met during January and February each year, which made for easy stories while it was in session. The rest of the year, however, I had to come up with something to fill a couple of minutes of news time each night.

Sometimes I went for a light feature story, like a visit to the Virginia State Fair, which allowed me to highlight such crowd favorites as the racing pigs, which are exactly what they sound like. Other times I would find obscure things or people and turn them into a story, like the time I saw a curious sign hanging from a building downtown, walked in, and ended up doing a package about a man who still made high-priced, custom violins by hand.

Governor Allen would often hold a public event, which I could cover and turn into a story. And on the days I had the chance to ask the governor a question or two, I tried to cover as many topics as I could to give me fodder for multiple pieces. Then, because legislative meetings were held regularly at the Capitol even when the entire legislature was not in session, I could get Democrats to provide their point of view on the same topics.

The whole scheme was beautiful, and here's how it worked. Let's say that on a Monday I got an interview with Governor Allen, a Republican. I could then grab some interviews with General Assembly Democrats, and the combination was enough material for a week's worth of stories.

The station usually wanted me to present my package live in the 6 p.m. show, which made the whole thing even easier. All I had to do was slap together a "donut" package of about a minute and then be ready to introduce it live on the air and then say a few words after it had run. (It was called a donut because it was the thing that was in the middle of my live speaking parts.)

The bottom line of all this is that I had about an hour's worth of work to do each day, just putting the package together for the news at 6 p.m. On most days, there was simply no need for me to arrive at work until mid-afternoon, and then I'd be finished as soon as I got off the air—usually by 6:15 p.m. This was an absolutely ideal schedule for a working alcoholic.

Before long, the work schedule merged with my drinking schedule, and both happened simultaneously. I could arrive at the Capitol bureau at a leisurely time and put my story together in just an hour or so. That left a good amount of time to sneak out to the Penny Lane Pub before my live shot.

The Pub was just a couple of streets away from the Capitol complex, so it was easy to slip over there to knock back some beers and Liverpool Kisses, which were shots that were the specialty of the house. A Liverpool Kiss was a mixture of schnapps and blackberry brandy, with a little dash of 151 rum on top so it can be set on fire before serving. You learned quickly to blow out the little blue flame right away, lest the rim of the shot glass get too hot.

I'd sit at the bar in the pub, chatting with proprietor Terry O'Neill and his brother-in-law and bartender Tommy Goulding—both charming lads from Liverpool—and pound beers and shots until it was time to rush back the Capitol and sit in front of the camera for the 6 p.m. show. I can't begin to estimate how many times I appeared on television screens throughout the Charlottesville area while significantly buzzed. Either I was exceptionally good at getting away with it, or my bosses had just decided to put up with it until something bad happened. After my hit, I could be back at the bar before the anchors tossed to the sports guy.

For the two months a year when the Virginia General Assembly was in town, the drinking only increased, and the community that sprang up around the legislative session became a sort of civilization of its own. There were cocktail parties almost every night, each hosted by a different industry lobbying group or trade association, and the printed calendar of these alcoholic events was a coveted road map to free drinks and food.

I can recall draining vodka and cranberry drinks at one such party held in the ornate atrium of Old City Hall, which is adjacent to Capitol Square. I stood next to a colleague as we both watched an extremely portly state senator load his plate with steamed shrimp.

"Look at him over there," my friend said. "He's committing shrimp genocide."

And even on the nights when there was a good party to get me liquored up, which was most of the time, I still always stopped at Penny Lane for a few before going home.

During this time in the mid-1990s, I met a woman named Tayne Renmark and we hit it off, even though I knew she was already married. I can see now that it was my alcoholic thinking and related behavior that allowed me to get involved with a married woman, because at the time I had no regard for what harm my actions might cause others. I think it is safe to say that if my lifestyle had been different, Tayne and I would never have gotten together and may never have even met. But as it happened, she soon divorced her first husband, we lived together for a number of years, and we got married in 2000.

6

On the Trump Campaign, My Past Catches Up
February 2019

In early January 2019, my old friend from Connecticut, Justin Clark, reached out to me. Since I'd met him on Linda McMahon's Senate race in Connecticut in 2012, he'd served as deputy national political director on the Trump campaign and had gone on to a senior position in the White House. He was moving to the re-election campaign as a senior advisor, along with fellow White House official Bill Stepien, and wanted to know if I'd had any "thoughts about joining the re-elect," as the campaign for a second term was sometimes called.

The thought had crossed my mind because, although I loved working for Sonny Perdue, my heart would always be with campaigns. I told Clark that I believed in President Trump's policies and leadership, and I would be thrilled to speak to someone about signing up for the re-elect.

I met with Raj Shah, the former principal White House deputy press secretary who was helping with initial staff hires. We talked about my experience on different campaigns and with national political committees, and I felt obliged to bring up my history with alcohol. Shah said that he thought it wouldn't be a problem as long as I was no longer drinking, especially because President Trump was aware of the power of alcohol. Shah told me that President Trump had always completely abstained from drinking, and that he blamed the disease of alcoholism for his brother Fred's death at the young age of forty-two in 1981.

"I think he'd see you as a story of redemption," Shah said.

We talked about a senior-level communications position in the campaign, and I said that I'd like it to be public facing, and one that interacted with the media as much as possible. I thought I was a strong writer, but I also thought I was good at handling reporter relationships, and I liked the idea of representing the president on television. Shah mentioned a deputy director position in communications, perhaps overseeing press staffers or the rapid response department. I asked about the job of national press secretary, but he said they already had someone in mind for that (I later learned that it was Kayleigh McEnany, who would indeed assume that role).

Although I had never been on a presidential campaign before, I thought I had proven myself to be a valuable asset through my work for Sonny Perdue at USDA. We had traveled the country promoting President Trump's agenda and accomplishments and rallied the support of rural America—the heart of Trump Country—for the president's cause.

In state after state, each trip resulted in strikingly favorable local coverage, which the White House clearly very much appreciated. I was told many times that our aggressive USDA model of travel and "earned media" was something they wished that other cabinet secretaries and departments would emulate. At one point, I was even asked to give a presentation to my counterparts in other executive branch departments to demonstrate how we planned a trip and squeezed every ounce of positive publicity for the administration out of it.

I knew, however, that the Department of Agriculture had some built-in advantages over other cabinet-level agencies in the Trump administration. First, it had a natural constituency that was easily identifiable—rural America and the farmers who lived and worked there. We could go into any state and have a perfectly legitimate, official reason to be there, while also generating local news that helped with the president's re-election. Not every cabinet department had such easy applicability to every state.

Additionally, we were armed with Sonny Perdue, a gifted politician who knew policy and exactly how to explain it to people, and who was adept at retail politicking as well. No one was better than Perdue at shaking hands and kissing babies at a state fair, while simultaneously extolling the merits of Trump administration priorities on local television.

All told, I felt that at that point in my career, and at age forty-nine, I was worthy of something a little higher in the campaign organizational chart than a slot that had the word "deputy" on it. I didn't say anything at the time, but I didn't know if I would ultimately accept the offer of such a position.

While the interview process was still unfolding, I spoke to Secretary Perdue about it, because he was a boss who I respected, and I valued his opinion.

"If they offer you a job and you take it, you'd better be ready for that to consume your life completely for the next two years," he said, knowing that I had a wife and two young children at home. "And your family has to be ready for that, too."

I had seen Brad Parscale, the Trump 2020 campaign manager, on *60 Minutes* and other network television shows, but I knew little about him when I went over to the campaign headquarters in Rosslyn, Virginia, to meet with him and Shah. The offices were in a steel-and-glass high-rise on the Virginia side of the Potomac River separating it from Washington, DC.

Parscale had been the digital guru of the 2016 campaign and was credited by many for having masterminded the use of Facebook and other online tools to sway voters in a way that was not easily detectible by Hillary Clinton's team or the national press. He was also six foot eight and had a personality to match his physical size.

I was already in the conference room with Shah when Parscale barged in (a guy who stands six foot eight doesn't "breeze in" anywhere), wearing a three-piece suit and acting like he had a thousand places he had to be at once. After a meeting that I thought was very brief—at most thirty minutes—Parscale left the room and I was alone with Shah again. After some small talk, he walked me to the elevator with a promise that he would be in touch.

Just a couple of days passed before my phone rang again.

"Listen, I know that we talked about certain jobs that we might consider you for, but what do you think about being the director?" Shah said.

"Director of what?" I asked.

"Of communications," Shah said. "Director of communications for the Trump campaign."

That sounded pretty good to me, and before the end of February 2019, I had started the job. On my first day, I walked around and explored the sizeable office a little. It was almost completely vacant and nothing like the bustling hive of presidential campaigning it would become over the next two years. In fact, it was empty and dark across much of the office, and it was surreal to walk from place to place as the motion sensors turned the lights on as I moved.

One of the first things that Parscale encouraged me to do was to hire an executive assistant, which was advice that I was repeatedly grateful for over the course of my time on the campaign. During the two years, I had three different assistants, who were invaluable in keeping my schedule straight, acquiring background for media hits, and making what seemed like constant travel arrangements.

Sonny Joy Nelson was my first hire, and I had noticed her résumé out of hundreds in a pile because of her first name, which had reminded me of the cabinet secretary for whom I had just worked. Sonny was fantastic and was promoted to other jobs in the campaign before long. Then there was Lyndee Rose, who did great work before following Kayleigh McEnany to the White House. And finally, there was Kimmy Hammond, who witnessed all the real turmoil of the later days in the campaign, up to and beyond Election Day, and who was a fantastic teammate when it seemed the whole world was out to sink us.

As I settled into the comms director job, I was still concerned every day that someone would try to make an issue of my alcoholic past, even though I had been assured by Parscale that everyone at the White House, including President Trump, was comfortable with it. My various arrests were a matter of public record, including two DUI convictions and the resulting jail time. Even though I was not the candidate myself, a record like that for a senior staffer on a presidential campaign could make for a good story in the right publication.

If someone did write a story, the problems with that would be many. Despite the assurances I had received from Parscale, there was no telling what the reactions would be once the information about my history was public. In my early days as the campaign's communications director, I knew very few people at the White House, and I had heard whispers that some who were close to the president weren't thrilled that I was selected for the job, either because I was mostly unknown and unproven, or because they had favored someone else for the position. An embarrassing story about my past alcohol abuse would not be a great way to start, and it would be an easy reason to push me out if someone so desired.

Then there was the fact that such a story about my past would be extremely troubling at home. Dena would hate the idea of my—our—private business being spilled across the pages of some newspaper. Worse than that would be the online spreading of the story, on Twitter and elsewhere, that might fade over time, but never truly go away in the replies and comments. Dena's family, who certainly knew I'd had a problem with alcohol, didn't know the extent of my legal troubles. And my own family would probably worry that such a situation would drive me back to drinking again.

It would be best if those stories were never written, for sure.

It didn't take long before I had to confront the issue head-on. In the first week of March 2019, I got an email from a reporter at a major newspaper in the northeastern US saying that the paper had received information about my background from a source. The email contained the highlights of my arrest record followed by a series of questions, including whether I had disclosed any of the information prior to being hired at USDA or on the campaign, and if I had ever sought treatment for alcohol abuse.

I had anticipated this conversation, whenever it came, and I got on the phone with the reporter for a preliminary off-the-record talk. First, I said, I was not the candidate, which is a key point. I was simply a campaign staffer, and therefore my past shouldn't be considered news-worthy. Second, these were old arrests and convictions, which had all occurred years before I had worked on the Trump campaign, or even in the Trump administration at USDA, for that matter. Third, I had been completely honest and forthcoming about my record with Secretary Perdue at USDA and then Brad Parscale at the campaign. Fourth, I was no longer drinking and had not touched alcohol since May 16, 2015 (nearly four years earlier at the time of this conversation). Fifth, I had indeed sought and received treatment for alcohol abuse (several times, in fact). And sixth, if my criminal history was fair game, then the media had better open the books for every senior staffer on every campaign, because there was no way I was the only one with an alcohol-related record.

The reporter listened politely and told me there would be a discussion with the editors. I didn't hold out much hope that I had killed the story, so I drafted a quote for myself that I would submit if I had to. I also texted Secretary Perdue to ask if he'd be willing to supply a quote of support as well, and he quickly agreed. Feeling like the ceiling was caving in on me, I told Parscale what was happening and also asked for, and received, a short quote from him, defending and expressing confidence in me.

Incredibly, the news came back from the reporter that the paper would not be writing the story. If I had not been forthcoming with the campaign or USDA, it might have been a different outcome, they said, but as it was, the story would not be published.

After the smoke cleared that day, I called Dena to tell her about the inquiry. It was good news that I had killed the story, but there would likely be more. Whoever was pushing it certainly wouldn't stop simply because one outlet had passed on it.

About a week later, I got another ominous email from a reporter I had known from my Richmond days, who was by then with a DC-based publication. It was the same stuff, basically the same questions, and obviously the same answers as the first time. I told Parscale that it was happening again, and I got on the phone with the reporter for the same conversation as with the first reporter. Once again, the response was that there would be an internal discussion with the editors.

After a brief, but excruciating, waiting period, my phone rang again.

"It's dead," the reporter said. "The editors decided not to run it. I should tell you that the story was basically written, but they've decided to hold it."

I breathed out a sigh and felt tension leave me. "Thank you," I said.

"But if anything else happens, we'll bring it back to life, I'm pretty sure," came the warning. "If there's another arrest or something, that would change everything."

"Of course it would," I said. "But that's not going to happen. And thanks."

I went to tell Parscale that the story had been killed, but when I found him, he already knew that because he'd had a very terse conversation with a different reporter at the same publication.

"I told them that if they were going to run a story attacking my comms director almost two years before the election, that's a terrible way to start," Parscale said. "I said that if they ran that story, they could forget about having access to anyone here, or at the White House."

It's true that one of the worst things he could do to a journalist was threaten access.

"Wow," I said, appreciative that he'd gone to bat for me so strongly. "Thank you for doing that."

Over the next few days, three more national publications reached out to me, asking the same questions. We managed to fight them all off, and I learned through my conversations with those reporters that my arrest record was being shopped around by a specific Democratic opposition research firm that typically looks into the backgrounds of Republican candidates for office. This time, however, the firm had trained its sights on me, as a senior Trump campaign staffer, and unfortunately my background was full of nuggets for it to mine.

"They don't like you very much," one reporter told me.

"Yeah, it's sort of their job to hate me," I said, reflecting on the tactics of the political industry as a whole.

Because of my experience with these attempted "hit piece" news stories, I developed a strong aversion to attacking the staff of any campaign. Naturally, a candidate is an appropriate target of criticism, and a staffer who says or does things that are germane to the campaign should be considered in bounds. But if information is of a personal nature, and is unrelated to the job, my default position is to leave campaign staff alone.

The crisis subsided and I didn't hear from any media about my past for a long time. But it wouldn't last forever.

More than a year later, the *New York Post* ran a story about various members of Joe Biden's family who had had scrapes with the law but never got any jail time for their misdeeds. The charges included DUIs and the act of racking up $110,000 on a stolen credit card, but none of the Biden relatives had experienced much in the way of consequences.

The War Room, an operation within my communications department on the campaign, was headed by Matt Wolking, a true political knife fighter with whom I really enjoyed working. He and his team drafted a press release blasting the Bidens for getting preferential treatment in the criminal justice system, and it appeared in my inbox for my approval.

My initial instinct was to shoot down the release in the interest of self-preservation, because publicly citing someone else's drunk driving arrests did not seem like something I should be party to, as someone twice convicted of the same crime. It also seemed to me that if we went after the Bidens on this topic, it would be an open invitation for someone to bring up my own problematic background with alcohol and law enforcement. There was no question that, at least as a personal matter, the safest thing to do would be to scuttle the release and not tempt fate.

However, if I killed a press release to protect myself from a topic that was personally risky, I would be letting my personal interests dictate how I did my job. I decided to tell the team to move forward with the press release, but not to go overboard in pushing it.

As I had feared, the press release generated a phone call from a newspaper about my background. This was a publication I had not heard from in the initial volley of inquiries on the subject, and the reporter explained that the editors had resisted the story the first time around because it didn't seem relevant. But, much like in a court case when one side opens a door the other side can walk through, they believed that our attack on Biden family legal troubles had created a reason to write about me.

Ali Pardo, who had been promoted to one of the deputy director slots in the communications department, helped me work the reporter on the story. She made the basic arguments that I had made to the media the year before, and I took on the claim that we had opened the door for the story by sending out the press release.

"You're attacking the Bidens for doing the same thing that you, personally, are guilty of," the reporter said. "That's why it's news now."

I replied that it was not the same thing at all, and I implored the reporter to recognize the distinction.

"We went after the Bidens because they mostly got away with what they did, and no one went to jail," I said, in what is now familiar commentary about the Biden family. "But the difference between them and me is that I did face consequences. I went to jail twice, for a total of fifteen days, I was on probation for three years, my driver's license was suspended, I paid fines, and I had one of those breathalyzer things on my car. I paid for what I did. The point of the press release is that the Biden family did not."

Amazingly, that argument carried the day, and I credit Ali Pardo (now Ali Black since getting married after the campaign) with a major assist in killing the story. That was the last time I was forced to deal with my past during the campaign.

Throughout the course of all of that, I was always armed with those statements of support from Brad Parscale and Sonny Perdue, but I never had to use them. Here they are now, a few years later, for the first time in print.

Parscale's statement would have been: "Tim was open with us about his history from the beginning. If they think they can use opposition research on our staff to hurt the president's campaign, they're wrong."

And Sonny Perdue would have said: "Tim was honest with me about his history when we first met, and he did an exemplary, professional job for us at USDA. 'Let he who is without sin cast the first stone,' is the way I look at it. His path is a success story in my book. I'll vouch for him any day of the week."

The statement I had prepared for myself was somewhat longer:

> Like millions of Americans, I suffered from the disease of addiction to alcohol. Through the support of my wife and family, exceptional treatment, and a strong recovery network, I managed to overcome my dependency. Over the past four years, I have been completely sober, served in senior roles on a congressional staff and for a cabinet member, and been entrusted with a Top Secret security clearance, for which I underwent a thorough background check.
>
> Every morning I thank God for my sobriety and the promises which have come true as a result, including a loving wife and two beautiful young children. Now, political operatives have chosen to make an issue of my struggle and have tried to capitalize on it by feeding it to the media in order to hurt President Trump.
>
> Nevertheless, my family and I view my story as one of triumph, and one of experience, strength, and hope. I was candid with the campaign about my past before I was hired, and I am grateful that the president and his team believe in redemption, which is but one of many reasons I am proud to work for his re-election.

I had also written an op-ed under my own name, for submission to a publication in the event that a story about my background ever did run. In it, I credited my wife and family for helping me through recovery from alcoholism, and thanked Representative Barletta, Secretary

Perdue, and President Trump for standing by me. And I lashed out at the people who were shopping around my shortcomings to the press:

> Unlike the millions of Americans who battle the same disease of addiction I faced, I also hold a senior position on the President Trump's re-election campaign, which unfortunately makes me a target of partisan Democrat operatives. These are people who seek to hurt the president by making public my own struggles and the problems with the law I faced as a result. In my estimation, that political opponents would use a campaign staffer's battle with addiction against the candidate himself says more about the people wielding the information than it ever could about me.

The fact that those stories never ran meant that I never had to use the op-ed or any of those quotes, and I'm grateful for that. It also preserved my ability to tell my story on my own terms, which I am doing through the publication of this book. In so doing, I am eliminating the possibility that some partisan hack could threaten me in the future with the release of my criminal record, because I am detailing it myself. And more important, by telling it this way, I stand the chance of helping another alcoholic who might read about my experience.

Some might wonder how I reconciled my feelings about my own addiction problems while I would attack Joe Biden's son, Hunter, who also has engaged in substance abuse struggles. The answer is that I never criticized him for his addictions, only the illicit business dealings that involved his father, and I will touch on that later.

7

Jumping into Politics
1999 to 2000

In Virginia, a governor can't serve consecutive terms, so at the end of
his four years in office in January 1998, George Allen was replaced by
fellow Republican Jim Gilmore, who had been elected after serving as
attorney general during Allen's term. Everyone suspected that Allen
would run for the US Senate in 2000 against incumbent Democrat
Chuck Robb, himself a former governor and the son-in-law of President Lyndon B. Johnson.

After six years at WVIR, with five of them in the Capitol bureau,
I was tired of local television news and wanted to shift gears. I
approached Governor Allen and his team, mentioned the expected run
for the Senate in 2000, and asked to be considered for the job of press
secretary if he did indeed mount a campaign. I had no idea if I had even
the slightest chance of being considered, but I was swinging from my
heels in case I hit it. By midyear 1999, I had been hired—given a tryout,
really—as the communications director for the Republican Party of
Virginia (RPV). I had been placed at RPV by Chris LaCivita, a veteran

GOP operative who was to be Allen's campaign manager for the Senate race the following year. It would not be the last time I worked with LaCivita over my career.

I suppose I must have been effective—or at least I caused no damage—because in the 1999 elections, the party helped Governor Gilmore to achieve Republican control of the entire General Assembly for the first time since the Civil War, and I got promoted to the Allen 2000 Senate campaign.

It was a tremendous experience for me as my first exposure to a real political campaign. The Allen 2000 Senate campaign was led by LaCivita as the campaign manager and Jay Timmons as chief of staff, the same title he'd held when Allen had been governor.

It was a race that I always felt like we were going to win, at the very beginning and at the very end, and on every day in between. The opponent, Chuck Robb, had once been a glamorous figure in Virginia— young and handsome, married to LBJ's daughter, and once considered a potential presidential candidate. Any race is tough against an incumbent, though, and it was not an easy fight.

Through the course of it, I can remember a few incidents that were alcohol-related and concerning.

Once, while we were on a multiweek tour of rural Virginia in a recreational vehicle, we spent the night in a hotel, which was a rare thing on the frugal Allen campaign. The hotel had a bar, and I drank there with some of the other campaign staff until they turned out the lights. This was risky for all of us, because Timmons had a set of rules on the campaign that governed campaign activity and personal behavior. I don't remember what Rule #1 was, but I know that Rule #2 strictly forbade the consumption of alcohol while representing the campaign.

Having violated Rule #2 all night long, and perhaps having offended the spirit of the rule worse than anyone else based on the volume of alcohol consumed, I overslept. Waking up to campaign aide Henry

Doggett banging on my door the next morning, I scrambled to get ready to depart. Surely stinking of booze, I was the last one to appear outside to climb aboard the RV. As I slumped into my seat, I caught a side-eye look from Allen as he assessed my condition. Neither he, nor anyone else, ever said anything about it.

Another time on a Monday morning at home in Richmond, I awoke to a hangover so bad that I was legitimately physically unable to get out of bed the next morning. I called in sick to work, which is something one should never do on a political campaign. LaCivita tried to call me once, but I didn't answer, and I had no other contact with anyone there until the next day.

There was an empty suite of offices on the same floor as the campaign's space in a downtown Richmond building. Some of us used it as a smoking lounge, and so I went there as soon as I got to work on Tuesday morning. LaCivita had gotten there before me and had a cigarette going with a steaming cardboard cup of coffee.

There were maybe a dozen cups like it scattered across a shelf at the window. Each one was filled with scores of spent cigarette butts. The place was a mess and it looked like it hadn't been cleaned by anyone for months.

"Morning," LaCivita said.

"Morning."

"Where were you yesterday?" he asked, and it sounded slightly accusatory.

I mumbled a lie I had prepared about a family health emergency.

LaCivita smoked silently for a few seconds. As he crushed out his cigarette and walked out of the room, he looked over his shoulder.

"You can't just disappear like that," he said, and was gone.

In the summer of 2000, the Republican National Convention was held in Philadelphia, and in an effort to save a little campaign cash, the decision was made that Governor Allen and I would stay at my parents' house in the suburbs (yes, really). But even that wasn't safe enough for me.

After a day spent in a hangover fog at the convention, I returned to my parents' place with Allen, who said he wanted to retire to his bedroom with the debate "playbook," a binder containing the detailed strategy we wanted to employ in the approaching first debate with Chuck Robb. Except that neither of us could find it.

After a few frantic phone calls to my Republican National Committee contacts, I gave up locating the playbook from afar and just hoped that it would surface the next day when we returned to the First Union Center, as the convention arena was called at the time. I found the binder under a table along "radio row"—where conservative talk show hosts were stationed—and actually let Allen think that he'd been the one who left it there. I didn't know whose fault it was, but as a staffer, it had been my job to keep track of such an important item. As I could say about many situations I found myself in during those days, it never would have happened if I'd been clearheaded.

By the end, Allen beat Robb by more than four and a half points, 52.3 percent to 47.7 percent, and became the next US Senator from the great Commonwealth of Virginia. As the campaign press secretary, I fully expected to be offered a job in the Senate office in Washington, DC, and I intended to accept it.

Time passed and I had not heard from Timmons, who, as the incoming chief of staff, was putting his team together. And then, one weekday I was out to lunch in Richmond with Henry Doggett from the campaign—rather he was eating lunch and I was drinking it—when Timmons called on my cell phone. This was in the early days of cell phones, and I remember wishing that he had not been able to reach me so easily.

Timmons invited me to come in to talk to him about a communications position in the Senate office. I asked him when he wanted to do that, and he said immediately, so I settled up with our waitress and left Doggett sitting in the diner. It took just a couple minutes to drive to the campaign office, and it wasn't long before I was sitting in front of Timmons in his office.

I was aware that I was pretty buzzed. Not hammered, but buzzed. And there I was, suddenly yanked into a job interview that I hadn't been expecting.

The only details I have retained from that conversation are that Timmons asked me how I envisioned the communications shop being structured in the Senate office. It wasn't a very difficult question, and it ought to have been easy to bluff my way through an answer without even trying very hard.

But in my slightly inebriated state, feeling as unprepared as I did, I didn't answer him right away. In fact, the beat that I took to gather myself turned into a moment, which became a pause that got longer, and it finally had to be described as a prolonged silence. My lack of speaking felt like a barrier that I couldn't break through, and the result was that I sat there staring at Timmons, not talking, for what felt like an hour.

But let's say it was just thirty seconds. That was bad enough, because he started talking again before I did.

"I figured after all this time, you'd have given this some thought," he said, and I knew that he knew that I was half loaded. Our conversation was over, and I left.

George Allen did go to Washington, DC, in January 2001 to be sworn in as a US Senator, and I never did receive an offer of employment in the office.

As I write about these events for this book and think about them in depth for the first time in more than twenty years, it occurs to me that this exchange with Jay Timmons was different from other conversations I'd had that were made difficult by alcohol. In the years that followed, I would get fired from several jobs for alcohol infractions, but this was probably the first time that I am certain that booze cost me a job before I had even been hired.

8

The Russia Hoax Dies
March 2019

On Sunday, March 24, 2019, Attorney General William Barr sent a four-page letter to the House and Senate Judiciary Committees, summarizing the "principal conclusions" of the report filed by Robert Mueller, the special counsel looking into allegations that the Trump campaign had colluded with Russia to win the 2016 election. I got a call from Brad Parscale that day with the marching order that the campaign had to seize on the letter and declare that the president had been completely cleared of all accusations of conspiring with agents of a foreign nation to win an American election.

We treated Barr's letter as declarative, and Trump tweeted a summation of his view late in the afternoon: "No Collusion, No Obstruction, Complete and Total EXONERATION. KEEP AMERICA GREAT!"

It's obvious to any fair observer that the first two years of the Trump administration were hijacked by the false Russia collusion narrative, invented by Democrats and pushed by their allies in the media.

It kept the White House on a defensive footing and occupied a lot of the time and energy of the president's re-election campaign.

Much importance was attached to Mueller's highly anticipated testimony before congressional committees in July 2019, but his appearances were, frankly, terrible. When those hearings fell flat, there was much celebration inside the campaign, as we felt that we could begin to put the issue behind us and plow ahead with re-election efforts. We now know that the "Steele dossier," on which much of the original collusion theory was based, was phony and paid for by Hillary Clinton's campaign.

We also know that one of the main antagonists in the Russia hoax fiasco, Democratic Representative Adam Schiff of California, was brazenly lying the whole time he was a ubiquitous presence on CNN, MSNBC, and the legacy networks on the matter. He claimed many times to have seen and possessed "smoking gun" evidence that would link Trump to a conspiracy with Russia to influence the 2016 election. And he was so convinced that the information contained in the Steele dossier was accurate that he read the whole thing into the Congressional Record.

Schiff delighted in propping up his empty accusations by cloaking them in the language of the House Intelligence Committee on which he sat, strongly implying that he knew a lot more than he could say because the information was "classified."

"I can't go into the particulars, but there is more than circumstantial evidence now," he said once on *Meet the Press* on NBC. It was never true, of course. Such evidence never existed, Schiff never produced anything, and the only thing that was proven was that he's a habitual liar and a partisan who is toxic to the political discourse in America.

He demonstrated his dishonesty in an appearance on ABC's *The View* in July 2019 after the Russia collusion narrative had been shut down, when he reversed himself on the claim that his proof was so secret that he couldn't even talk about it.

"Can you share with us right here, right now on *The View*, the evidence that you have and explain why Mueller was wrong yesterday?" Schiff was asked by co-host Meghan McCain.

Amazingly, Schiff replied that the evidence was always "in plain sight, not hidden anywhere," since he could no longer allude to fictional proof that only he had seen.

Well after the 2020 election, Schiff was again a guest on *The View* and was pressed to acknowledge his ocean of lies by guest host Morgan Ortagus. His defense, basically, was that it wasn't his fault if the Steele dossier was full of fake information.

But Schiff's assault on the truth went beyond the Russia hoax. On another occasion, he lied when he denied that his staff had made contact with a whistleblower involved in the first Trump impeachment.

And another time in a committee hearing, when describing a phone call involving President Trump and Volodymyr Zelenskyy, the president of Ukraine, Schiff quoted parts of the conversation that *did not occur*. Incredibly, he literally made up passages, and then cast them as things that Trump had said.

"I have a favor I want from you, though," Schiff said in the hearing, hoping that people believed that he was quoting President Trump from a transcript of the phone call. "And I'm going to say this only seven times, so you better listen good. I want you to make up dirt on my political opponent. Understand? Lots of it, on this and on that."

Only, Trump had said nothing of the sort, and nothing that was anything close to "I want you to make up dirt on my political opponent."

It was a wild fabrication, intended to mislead people who were watching the hearing, and it was purposeful. Before the hearing was even over, Schiff was exposed as having invented parts of the conversation, and he then said that his remarks had been "parody."

But the only parody was Schiff's own performance, as he was like a cartoon version of a sanctimonious member of Congress who claimed to care about the truth. His own insatiable appetite for dirt on his political opponents, and more specifically, on Donald J. Trump, was exposed in 2018 when audio tapes emerged capturing Schiff eagerly talking to people who had identified themselves as foreigners promising salacious information on Trump.

According to the *Daily Mail*, two Russian comedians duped Schiff into thinking that they were Ukrainian officials who possessed compromising pictures of Trump with a reality television star. They also told Schiff that they had recordings of a meeting between a Trump aide and a known Russian spy at a mafia-connected joint in Brooklyn that did not actually exist. And Schiff had even thought to warn the jokesters that the Russians could be listening to the call, saying, "I would caution that our Russian friends may be listening to the conversation so I wouldn't share anything over the phone that you wouldn't want them to hear."

Schiff, of course, later claimed that he knew the call had been "bogus," but the audio of the eight-minute conversation only supported one conclusion—that he had been taking it seriously and had hoped to obtain the materials that he believed would be harmful to Trump. A member of Schiff's staff even followed up with an email to the Russian comedians under the belief that they were representatives of Ukraine's parliament, saying the conversation had been "productive."

The best part of this story was the exposure of Schiff as an enormous hypocrite. After all, he had spent two years claiming that Trump had colluded with Russians, yet he had been caught seeking damaging information on a political opponent from people described to him as foreign nationals. A person with shame would have felt some after this episode, however I doubt Schiff is capable of that.

In June 2023, House Republicans censured Schiff, the worst admonishment available to them short of expulsion from the chamber, for these offenses and more. By then, Schiff's antics had probably been forgotten by many Americans, but in 2019 much of it was still fresh.

Four days after Barr's letter dropped in March 2019, I traveled to Grand Rapids, Michigan, for my first Trump rally as the campaign's communications director.

"The Russia hoax is finally dead," Trump said to the loud crowd at Van Andel Arena. "The collusion delusion is over."

And he relished taking a victory lap.

"The special counsel completed its report and found no collusion and no obstruction. I could have told you that two and a half years ago very easily," Trump said. "Total exoneration. Complete vindication. You know, it's interesting Robert Mueller was a god to the Democrats. He was a god to them until he said there was no collusion."

I attended that rally with Kayleigh McEnany, who had been chosen by the president himself to serve as the campaign's national press secretary on my staff, and Erin Perrine, who oversaw the deputy and assistant press secretaries as one of my deputy communications directors. For a portion of Trump's remarks, we sat on the front edge of the press riser because it was a head-on vantage point that was above the heads of the crowd on the floor of the arena. The three of us didn't know each other very well, so we mostly listened to the president and people watched.

The crowd was large, energetic, and in full voice. Both seating levels of the arena were full, as was the large floor space between the stage and press area. Behind the president were full bleachers topped by a massive American flag. On either side of the big flag were red rectangles, at least thirty feet long, emblazoned with the campaign messaging of the time, "JOBS! JOBS! JOBS!" in white capital letters. As always with a Trump rally, the production value was top shelf.

As he usually did, Trump spent some time and energy bashing the media, disparaging them consistently throughout his remarks. He referred to the Russia collusion hoax, which we now know it undeniably was, as a "crazy attempt by the Democrat party and the fake news media right back there" to undo his election victory in 2016.

When he referred to the media at the back, sometimes gesturing in the direction of the riser on which we were sitting, many in the crowd would turn and look while they were booing. From the glowering looks on a lot of the faces, it was clear that the Trump crowd did not hold the assembled members of the media in the highest esteem.

It occurred to me that none of the people in the crowd knew who I was or that I was the communications director for President Trump's campaign. All they could see was a guy in a suit sitting on the media riser, and so I imagined they assumed that I was a reporter. I must admit, it was an uncomfortable feeling having so many people shout angrily in my direction, and it wasn't long before the three of us found another place to watch.

From that point forward, I only visited the press riser if I had a television hit to do before the president's speech, or if I needed to speak to a specific reporter. And during the dozens of Trump rallies that I attended over the next two years, I never sat on the riser during the president's remarks again.

9

The RNC and Richmond Again
2001 to 2004

With no job in the Senate to slide into, it was my good fortune that Virginia governor Jim Gilmore had become the chairman of the Republican National Committee (RNC) in Washington, DC. I was able to land a job there quickly, thanks to the Virginia connection, although looking back, it might not have been the best thing for my ever-growing drinking problem.

If I had gone jobless for a spell after the Allen campaign, it might have dawned on me that something had to give. Instead, I carried on under the illusion that I could just keep doing what I was doing.

I very quickly made myself comfortable in Bullfeathers, a popular Capitol Hill bar on the next block over from the RNC. A small group of us retired there every afternoon for a good, solid drinking session before heading home. We took to calling it the RNC Annex, because at any given moment there might be enough Republican Party employees present to hold a staff meeting at the bar.

It was the same old deal for me. Go to work with a hangover, suffer through the day at far below 100 percent effectiveness, trudge to the bar for happy hour, and stagger home to pass out before doing it again the next day. Some mornings, I walked to the Rosslyn Metro stop from my Virginia apartment instead of driving to Capitol Hill, and when the weather was warm, I'd work up a decent sweat. With my history of emitting noticeable alcohol fumes after boozing, I doubt there could be anyone on the subway car with me who didn't know what I'd been up to the night before.

One time at work after a meeting broke up, RNC communications director Mark Miner pulled me aside after everyone else was gone and said, "Let me ask you, do you drink every day?"

I stammered that I didn't think it was every day, but probably three or four days a week. He looked at me, clearly not believing my low-ball description of my alcoholic intake, and just nodded. I left before the conversation could continue.

One bright and sunny Tuesday morning, September 11, 2001, was like any other day as we all headed to work. I can remember walking into the RNC communications department and seeing people huddled around television monitors. Someone explained that an airplane had crashed into the World Trade Center, and I could see the images of the smoking tower on the screens. That had been American Airlines Flight 11.

After just a few minutes, a second plane, United Airlines Flight 175, hit the other tower and we all realized instantly that the first impact had not been an accident. Before long, someone yelled that some news organizations were reporting that there had been an explosion of some sort at the Pentagon, which we would learn had been yet another airplane—American Airlines Flight 77.

Looking out the window, we could see hundreds of people streaming down the streets of Capitol Hill, as the House office buildings nearby had been evacuated. After just a few minutes more, the RNC announced that we were evacuating as well. All of us were confused and frightened as we found ourselves standing on the street among the crowds of people seemingly fleeing in all directions.

The city had stopped all public transportation, including Metro service, leaving us with limited options. A coworker suggested that we go to her apartment, which was a small English basement place nearby on Capitol Hill, so we made for her car. As we were climbing into her vehicle, the air seemed to fracture with the sound of an explosion all around us. It was like the sensation you get when a lightning strike happens so close to you that the thunderclap is nearly simultaneous, deafening, and terrifying. We reflexively ducked, not knowing what further calamity was possible after what we had seen on television already that morning.

As the initial sound blast receded, it was replaced by the distinct roar of powerful airplane jet engines, and we realized that we'd been hit with a sonic boom caused by fighter jets passing overhead. It was an unusual thing to witness in Washington, DC, where much of the city is a no-fly zone.

Because we had priorities, we stopped at a corner convenience store near the apartment to buy several cases of beer, and thankfully the proprietor had not decided to close and evacuate as well. We piled into the apartment, which felt a little bit safer because it was partly underground, and we drank and watched the television news coverage. It was hard to get cell phone calls to go through, as we tried to reach family and friends outside of DC, because it seemed that all the cell towers were getting overwhelmed.

I remember Tom Brokaw telling his NBC audience that there was another plane being tracked coming up the Potomac River toward Washington, DC. Now I think that he was probably describing the one that the heroic passengers aboard a fourth plane, United Airlines

Flight 93, brought down in Pennsylvania. Members of my family think that those people saved our lives, because we were at least vaguely in the vicinity of the terrorists' ultimate target, whether it was the White House or the US Capitol.

And I remember that the day provided an excuse to throw off the brakes on my drinking. The United States was under attack by an as-yet unknown enemy, so why shouldn't I get as drunk as possible? It was a familiar and routine conversation I had with myself over the years, with an endless series of reasons, varying between legitimate and lame, that I employed to give myself permission to drink, over and over.

After many hours, the city began to awake from its emergency shutdown, and the Metro announced that it was running again. I made it back to Virginia for the night and returned to work in the morning to take in the moving sight of an American flag hanging from every window on the RNC's façade. I remember staffers staying mostly silent, and talking in near whispers when they did have to speak. If September 11 had been chaotic and scary on Capitol Hill, September 12 was quiet and eerie.

But the work of the RNC went on, until one day near the end of November, when I got an email with instructions to come to an RNC all-staff meeting featuring remarks from Governor Gilmore. Moments after I received that message, I got another one that invited me to a meeting with Gilmore in the chairman's office. I noticed the other recipients of the second email and saw that it was a bunch of us who had come to the RNC from Virginia.

I forwarded the Virginia group email to Miner, the comms director, and asked him what the meeting was about. He replied, "Might be a good time to update your résumé."

And so it was that on Friday, November 30, 2001, Governor Gilmore announced that he was stepping down as RNC chairman, effective in mid-January of the following year, citing a schedule as chairman that was draining on his family life. Not-so-quiet speculation was that Gilmore did not see eye to eye with President George W. Bush's top political guy, Karl Rove, and that they had competing visions for the direction of the party and role of the chairman.

Without a job in DC to keep me there, it meant that I was headed back to Richmond, which was fine with me, because a period of time without work meant there was nothing to interfere with my drinking schedule.

*   *   *

When I got back to Richmond, I established a new home bar.

Poe's Pub on Main Street was an awesome spot, with a bunch of locals who could be counted on to drink at the same time every day. They joked that Church Hill, which was where Patrick Henry had delivered his "Liberty or Death" speech in 1775, was "a drinking neighborhood with a historical problem," and they took pride in living where they lived.

Proprietor Mike Britt and his wife, Jennifer, were good friends to everyone in the neighborhood, and Poe's Pub really became the physical heart of the community for me. With some of the other regulars, we formed a fake members-only organization within the bar, which we called the Platinum Club, and we pretended to be the elite elders who ruled over the establishment. My typical round that I ordered at the bar was a pint of Miller Light and a kamikaze shot.

Professionally, of course, I was humbler because I needed a job. Thankfully, Virginia's political calendar smiled on me again because there had been an election in November 2021 and a fellow named Jerry Kilgore had been elected attorney general, the only Republican to win statewide office. I had known Kilgore a little when he'd served as secretary of public safety in the Allen administration, and after a series of meetings with his team, and then him, I was hired to be the communications director for the Office of the Attorney General.

While it wasn't a national political gig any longer, it sounded pretty impressive, and it had a good long-term outlook because everyone knew that Kilgore was planning to run for governor in 2005. So, I basically had a four-year job, even if we lost the governor's race down the road. It was a little ironic, I acknowledged to myself, to be working for the top law enforcement officer in the state, while I had the lifestyle I did.

Around that time I acquired a special license plate because of my previous work with George Allen. I don't know if Virginia still does this, but in those days, each governor could issue a series of special license plates to friends and allies. The best feature is that if a police officer runs the tag number, it comes up blank in the computer, with even the driver's name kept out of the system. At least that's what I had heard.

After midnight one Thursday night, I was driving home from a buddy's poker game in Church Hill, having consumed probably seven or eight beers while playing cards. Feeling safe and insulated in our little neighborhood, I was rolling through stop signs on my simple half-mile drive to my house when I saw the flashing blue lights in my mirror.

Crap. The cop came to my window and I gave him my license and registration.

"Have you been drinking tonight, sir?" he asked me, and I replied that I had not. He told me to shut the car off and sit tight, and he walked back to his vehicle with my documents.

After a long while he returned and seemed somewhat perplexed.

"Sir, do you work for the government?" he asked.

I said that I did work for the attorney general, but that I guessed that he was actually talking about what happened when he ran my tag. I explained about the special plate.

"Are you headed home to this address?" he asked, handing me back my license and registration.

"Yes," I said.

"Go there right now, park this car, and do not drive it again until morning," he said. "You got that?"

I affirmed that I did, and I waited for him to drive off before I started my car and headed to Poe's Pub for a night cap.

As part of my job for Attorney General Kilgore, I often accompanied him on official visits and meetings if there was likely to be media present. Most of the time, a younger staff member would drive the official state vehicle for us, but there was one time when I was called on to drive Kilgore on a Monday morning.

It was unfortunate timing, because it followed an hours-long Sunday night session of indoor laser-tag at a local facility, which naturally involved a lot of drinking. Inside the laser arena, there were players of all ages running around in the dark, with strobe lights and smoke machines going crazy. Half drunk, I was slowly backing down a ramp with my laser gun at the ready, waiting for someone to rush at me from the gloom. I didn't see the kid crouched down behind me, looking around a different corner. I fell backwards over him and cracked the back of my skull on the cement floor.

The next morning, sick with a hangover and feeling a splitting headache from my fall, I showered and dressed early and headed to work for what I knew would be a spectacularly awful day.

I climbed behind the wheel for the drive with Kilgore down to Lynchburg or someplace, with a Diet Coke as my only life preserver. We got on the road, and I concentrated on keeping the car pointed straight and keeping my eyes open. The attorney general spent most of his time on the phone.

There came a point where Kilgore said that he was hungry, so we pulled off the highway and found a fast food drive-through. As we waited in line, I leaned my head back against the head rest and closed my eyes. The next thing I knew, Kilgore was elbowing me awake and saying my name loudly.

"You were really out for a minute there," he said. "You okay?"

I explained how I had hit my head the night before, while failing to mention all the beers I had drunk. He looked at me carefully and decided that I was not a safe driver at the moment and relieved me of my wheel duties.

When we returned to Richmond, I went home and straight to bed and didn't return to work for two more days.

10

 **COVID-19
2020**

On January 9, 2020, the World Health Organization (WHO) announced that it was tracking strange coronavirus cases originating in Wuhan, China. From my perspective, the WHO would incinerate all of its credibility as a public health entity over the coming months as it plainly tried to obscure China's culpability in the pandemic—but at the early stages, it still had the veneer of authority. Inside Trump 2020 headquarters, these news bulletins from the other side of the world were noticed, but life went on as usual on the campaign treadmill.

Less than two weeks later on January 20, the Centers for Disease Control and Prevention (CDC) began screenings at New York's JFK airport, San Francisco International, and Los Angeles International, because those three airports received the most passengers who originated in Wuhan. On January 31, President Trump restricted travel from China and it was clear to all of us that the virus was going to be a major problem, not just in the campaign, but everywhere.

I can clearly remember flying back to Washington, DC, from a Trump rally in February 2020 and connecting at O'Hare in Chicago. Perhaps as many as a quarter of the people in the airport were wearing masks. It was unsettling, and as I stood with our campaign traveling party at American Airlines Gate H1A, there was murmuring among us that the coronavirus was creeping up in significance and that everything was about to change.

With every passing day, the pressure grew from the media to suspend normal campaign activities in deference to the spreading virus. As I discussed an upcoming rally with Megan Powers, the campaign's director of operations, we went over all the precautions that the advance teams were taking, which protections would be offered to rally attendees, and other details that had become necessary.

"This just isn't sustainable," I said.

"Nope," she agreed.

Large, loud, boisterous rallies with thousands of supporters were a staple of the Trump campaign going back to his first run for the White House in 2015 and 2016. In many ways, they were the engine that made the rest of the campaign go, because they excited the base, drew media attention in key markets in key states, and gave the campaign the opportunity to vacuum up massive amounts of voter data through the registration of rallygoers.

President Trump, naturally, was reluctant to suspend this vital campaign activity, but eventually the COVID-19 reality of 2020 was impossible to deny. In the second week of March, the president consented to, and the campaign began canceling events, including rallies, voter coalition programs, and fundraising gatherings. In one twenty-four-hour period, the campaign announced a "Catholics for Trump" event in Milwaukee and then canceled it.

The media, choosing sides as ever, gave the Trump campaign far more grief about the safety of public events than they did the Biden campaign, even from the very beginning. As the months crept by, the president took a visible, public role in the government's efforts against the virus, but the media still wanted to nitpick about Trump rallies, and only Trump rallies.

Despite the fact that Nancy Pelosi had promoted San Francisco's Chinatown as a good place to go to support local businesses, the media singled out Trump as the only one subject to criticism. Joe Biden held eight campaign rallies (such as they were) in March 2020, six of them after the Trump rallies had ceased. And still the media harped on Trump as being a singular threat to public health.

On April 19, 2020, the *Wall Street Journal* ran an opinion piece by journalist Dave Seminara that encapsulated the issue perfectly and pushed back on early criticisms that Trump had not done enough to protect the country from the global pandemic:

> The Trump-acted-too-late story line would be more convincing if Mr. Biden and other Democrats had called for bolder action early in the crisis, but they didn't. Democratic candidates held five televised debates, lasting nearly 11 hours from Jan. 14 through March 15. They offered no policy proposals that haven't already been enacted and said little about the virus in the four events in January and February.

Inside the campaign, we all sensed how Democrats and the media would be teaming up to lay the blame for COVID-19 at President Trump's feet, and we prepared to fight back as best we could. I had been convinced that the strong economic conditions the nation had been enjoying throughout his term would carry the president through to victory, even if the race turned out to be close. But the pandemic changed everything.

"Now with the nation's economy reeling, more than 10 million Americans out of work and the stock market plummeting 30%, Trump and his aides are struggling to find a new message he can take to Americans for the November election," reported the *Los Angeles Times*, relating that the campaign's Facebook advertising was gingerly testing messaging that said Trump was uniquely positioned to keep America safe. "Whether voters agree with that argument, and how they view his competence in battling the coronavirus outbreak and reviving the ravaged economy, will probably determine his political fate, overwhelming other judgments about his rocky tenure in office. Polls show he faces widespread concern that he mismanaged the government's early response."

Well, of course polls might say that after months of media coverage blaming Trump for every death, even though the virus itself had its origins in China. CNN began logging COVID-19 deaths on a tracker that was almost always visible on screen, with numbers that ticked inexorably upward. Reporters and pundit panels dissected the president's every word and relentlessly bashed him over messaging or mask wearing for hours every day.

The news media hyped projected shortages in equipment and supplies that cities and states estimated they would need to fight the virus, maintain hospitals, and keep essential operations running. They insisted that President Trump communicate better with the public, and then demanded that he stop participating in the daily White House coronavirus briefing.

Many in the media, who had initially reported accurately that the virus had come from China, suddenly reversed themselves and declared it racist to pinpoint the origin of the pandemic. You couldn't say that it was likely that the virus escaped from a lab in Wuhan either, because that was deemed discriminatory as well.

The clear strategy was to prevent voters from having an alternate target for their frustrations over the virus. No, the media wanted the blame squarely affixed on the White House, despite the fact that every nation on earth had been horribly affected by the pandemic. The media despised Trump already and wanted him to lose, and a worldwide health catastrophe was the perfect weapon with which to bludgeon him.

The situation was also ideal for Biden politically, because running around the country campaigning for president was the last thing his team wanted him doing. He holed up at home in Wilmington, Delaware, and did his voter outreach from his basement with a television camera and teleprompter. He was terrible at it, the production quality was often poor, and the frequent bloopers and technical difficulties were unintentionally hilarious. Still, it was an advantage for him, because it protected him from public speaking and from voter interaction, which was where he was notoriously likely to do damage to himself. Additionally, we felt that many Americans were not aware of how significantly Biden's mental and physical faculties had eroded, and the basement strategy helped to keep that under wraps.

Dr. Anthony Fauci of the National Institute of Allergy and Infectious Diseases emerged as a near deity for reporters, and he quickly became a darling of the corporate media as a diminutive anti-Trump. At the same time, New York governor Andrew Cuomo also emerged as a media heartthrob, another Trump foil, as his state faced a complicated coronavirus situation. Cuomo had it all, as far as the media were concerned: a famous last name in Democratic Party politics, good looks, good television presence, and a willingness to throw political punches. Best of all, he was not Donald Trump.

The term "Cuomosexual," apparently first coined in a "coronavirus crush" song by an internet comedian called Randy Rainbow, took off as a word to describe the love and devotion that leftists felt for the governor of New York. Late-night talk show host Stephen Colbert used the word on the air, and Cuomo himself appeared on the Ellen DeGeneres show. Celebrities who publicly expressed their abiding affection for Cuomo included Jada Pinkett Smith and Chelsea Handler. Urban Dictionary even added a Cuomosexual definition as, "someone who has a deep, abiding affection, or attraction bordering on obsession, for a person carrying the surname Cuomo."

Cuomo went on to publish a book, unironically titled *American Crisis: Leadership Lessons from the COVID-19 Pandemic*, which he had to have been writing while the pandemic was in full swing, and for which he was paid more than $5 million. Left unclear was which "leadership" principle Cuomo was following when he ordered New York nursing homes to accept COVID-positive patients, which resulted in widespread deaths in the facilities. It was later revealed that he had underreported nursing home deaths by as much as 83 percent. But that's not what got him in trouble, since it all came crashing down when he resigned from office, rather than face impeachment, over a massive sexual harassment scandal.

The relentless assaults on President Trump by the media had their effect, and his standing in the polls worsened. A campaign that I had thought would be won with an offense based on a strong economy would instead have to be salvaged in a fight over blame for a worldwide health calamity.

In the years since, the Left has sustained its criticisms of Trump's COVID-19 response, and some fellow Republicans have criticized his handling of Fauci, vaccines, or the virus generally. But no one can convince me that anyone could have done better under similar, unprecedented circumstances.

11

Drinking, Campaigns, and Drinking
2005 and 2006

When 2005 rolled around, a bunch of us left the Office of the Attorney General and moved to the campaign for governor, where Jerry Kilgore would run against Democratic lieutenant governor Tim Kaine. Even though I had had the title of communications director for the attorney general's office, I was only called the press secretary on the campaign, which is a step down in hierarchy and in implied seniority. I later learned it was because senior campaign officials had concerns about my drinking habits and doubts about my management capabilities as a result.

Those senior campaign officials were right to question my focus because my drinking was steadily climbing. I made an appearance at Poe's Pub almost every night, and my personal finances were really beginning to suffer. I didn't have a credit card to my name, so I paid cash for everything. And when it got to be within a few days of payday every two weeks, I would often write a check for bar tabs and gamble that it wouldn't go through until after the direct deposit had appeared in my account.

I made sure that I had sufficient funds to keep my alcohol intake going, but actual financial responsibilities took much lower priority. None of these behaviors made me particularly popular at home, and I was forever making it worse.

One night after getting particularly smashed, I decided to take a hot bath when I got home from the bar, but I fell asleep in the tub and the water overflowed onto the floor. I awoke to Tayne's pounding on the door, which I had locked, because water was running out from under the bathroom door, out into the hall, and down to the first floor.

After I got dried off and dressed, I wordlessly gathered up some things, drove out to the campaign office in the small hours of the morning, and slept the rest of the night at my desk. For three days I didn't go home, instead sleeping at the office and using the bathroom there to wash up each morning. I don't know if any of my coworkers ever noticed.

As part of our campaign efforts, we had to put together an all-encompassing plan to present to the RNC and the White House and make it convincing enough for President George W. Bush to green-light millions of dollars in political spending on our behalf. It was my job to oversee the writing of the communications section of this campaign plan and to see that it was incorporated into the overall document.

It was here that my lack of focus, due to being hungover and preoccupied with my next drink, cost me.

After I had completed the first draft of the comms plan, I needed to circulate it among the campaign leadership for their review and edits. I attached the document to an email and filled in the names of recipients in the "To" window.

Typing a few letters of each name into Outlook, I selected the names of the campaign staffers to receive it: campaign manager Ken Hutcheson, campaign director Chris Nolen, special advisor Joey Carico, and my deputy, Tucker Martin.

After I had sent it, I turned my attention to something else, but after only a few moments, Nolen appeared at my office door.

"Dude, check the names you sent that to," he said. My body went cold as I pulled up the sent folder in my email.

As I had typed in the first letters of Martin's first name—T-U-C-K—I had selected the first option that appeared, which was not Tucker Martin but Tucker Carlson, who was appearing on political talk shows on CNN and MSNBC at the time.

I tried recalling the email, which never works in my experience, and then resorted to sending Carlson another email explaining what had happened and imploring him to delete the first one without opening the attachment. At least, I thought, he was on our side politically and might want to avoid doing anything to hurt our campaign.

He replied quickly, promising to delete the email, but didn't say anything about not opening the attached file. In another email a minute later, he had pulled out a detail from the comms plan and explained how he disagreed with it, thereby demonstrating that he had read at least part of the document.

I replied that I hoped that he could forget that the mishap had ever happened, and he assured me that he would. I never heard about it again, but those were a pretty harrowing couple of minutes.

One highlight that I recall was getting a quote published that was what press secretaries used to call the holy grail of communications. As the first gubernatorial debate between Kilgore and Kaine approached, the *Washington Post* was doing a preview story that examined how the two campaigns were preparing for the race. We wanted to raise expectations for Kaine's performance, because he was widely regarded as the better orator of the two.

I praised Kaine's skills: "Tim Kaine is a trial lawyer, well known as a smooth talker," I told the *Post*. "People say he's Clintonian in his debating style. He's a master debater, so we're certainly taking it seriously."

It was the magic phrase—"master debater"—that made it a sneaky joke about the opponent. It sounds, of course, like "masturbator," and is a great example of the sort of juvenile humor that campaign operatives love. To slip that past the reporter and his editors, and to actually get it into print, is something that I doubt I will ever match again.

We would lose that governor's race to Tim Kaine, and I'll never forget what Kilgore said when he addressed the campaign staff right before he went out to give his concession speech. He talked about the importance of winning versus losing: "I don't want anyone in this room to ever forget how it feels right now, because we lost. Yes, it's good that we tried hard, but we don't let our kids play soccer in leagues that don't keep score, because winning matters. So, thank you for your hard work, but please don't forget this feeling. Because winning matters."

After that race, I took a position as campaign manager for incumbent Republican representative Thelma Drake in the Tidewater area that included Norfolk and Virginia Beach. It was the first time I'd done anything outside the lane of communications, but I would have a lot of guidance from the consultants who were working on that 2006 campaign.

As part of the job, I had to live near the campaign office, which was about an hour and a half down I-64 from Richmond, meaning that I'd again be living and working in a different city from where my wife and home were. It was becoming such a common occurrence that neither one of us really blinked an eye, which was a bad sign for the marriage.

The last weekend before I was to move down to Tidewater, I predictably got ripped at Poe's Pub and ended my stay there by falling off a bar stool. I whacked the side of my face pretty hard on the tile floor when I fell, and it cut the corner of my eye fairly deeply, creating a wound that bled a lot. I didn't go to the emergency room or anything, and I didn't seek stitches. I just went home, put a Band-Aid on it, and hoped for the best.

When I got to the Drake campaign a few days later, I started telling people that I had been injured playing touch football when I knocked heads with a guy from the other team. Most people seemed to buy that, or at least stopped asking questions about it.

I got to know the campaign staff, which was quite small, and some of the staff of the official House office as well. I spoke frequently to the staffers from the DC office, many of whom were just voices on the phone. There was one in particular who I thought probably hated me the most, Dena Kozanas the legislative director, because I asked her so many stupid questions about the bills that Congress was voting on.

After hours, I was really beginning to push the limits of tolerance for my behavior, testing how far I could go before I really got into trouble. One night I was so drunk that the worker at a McDonald's drive-through window called the police on me, but the officer allowed me to park my car and call a campaign staffer to come pick me up.

A few days later a reporter told me he'd heard about the incident, but couldn't find a police report, so he couldn't write a story about it. I just shrugged my shoulders and said nothing.

Day drinking was back as well, and I began to stop on my way to work to buy a six-pack of beer or a four-pack of wine coolers. I'd leave them in the car in the parking lot and duck out once in a while to chug one down. I added wine coolers to the mix because I thought they were less visually identifiable as an alcoholic drink than a can of beer. That was disproven a few months later when one of our campaign workers told me that he'd heard that I'd been seen drinking a cooler while driving.

On election night 2006, I got so drunk that I had to stop talking to the media before the polls closed, and I don't remember the end of the night. We did win, however.

Regardless of the condition in which I finished the campaign, on paper it looked like a fine achievement. The 2006 election was a bloodbath for Republicans all over the place, but we had won in a difficult race that had been targeted by national Democrats. So, while Democrats had won enough seats to make Nancy Pelosi the speaker of the House for the first time, we had protected our little piece of turf in southeastern Virginia, so I had that going for me.

But even with that compelling victory on my stat sheet, the next political gig didn't fall in line like jobs usually had for me. Though I tried to push it out of my mind as a possibility, I had to consider that word was beginning to spread that my value to a campaign no longer outweighed the risks associated with my drinking.

With no steady work arriving, I began to euphemistically call myself a political consultant and I spent a few months idle. I finally persuaded the top aide to the speaker of the House of Delegates to contract with me on a monthly basis, and I wrote some press releases and remarks. At the same time, I did some minor campaign work for a handful of members of the state House, all of which managed to bring in enough income to keep me in drinking money. Most months, as usual, I contributed little to the upkeep of our household.

At about this time, it became clear that my marriage to Tayne was no longer functional in any way, and I decided that Richmond was no longer for me. I gathered as much stuff as I could fit in my car and I drove up to Northern Virginia, with a plan to stay on my cousin Brian Walton's couch until I could figure out what to do. I would be officially divorced before the end of 2008.

12

 ## Tulsa
June 2020

By June 2020, President Trump was itching to get back to the campaign trail and his trademark rallies. Selecting a location was an important decision because it had to be somewhere with extremely permissive COVID-19 regulations to allow a large indoor gathering in an arena setting. There weren't many cities and states that qualified, and even fewer that would welcome the crowd of thousands that came with a Trump rally.

Tulsa, Oklahoma, was ultimately selected. It wasn't a battleground state for sure—Trump beat Hillary Clinton there by more than thirty-six points in 2016—but it had a Republican governor and, in terms of COVID-19 restrictions, was considered the most open state in the country. Plus, the mayor of Tulsa was a Republican. It was the best situation possible under the pandemic circumstances.

When we announced the rally by press release, as we always did, there was an almost immediate explosion of criticism of the date chosen—June 19—the same day that Juneteenth is observed as the anniversary of the emancipation of slaves in America in 1865. I had known about Juneteenth because I had seen celebrations in Richmond before, and I always thought that the freeing of all slaves was an event worthy of being heralded. I knew that it was observed across the South, especially in Texas where it began, but I had never known it to be a nationally regarded day when all political campaign activity had to cease.

Nevertheless, with collective moral outrage, the national news media declared that it was a gross insult to the African American community for the president to hold a political rally on that day. This was despite the fact that even a brief internet search produced a ton of examples of Democrats holding normal political events on that same date through the years.

Additionally, the media revived an incident from Tulsa's history of racist violence, citing an event that had occurred ninety-nine years earlier as evidence that the city itself was a poor choice for a political event of the nature of a Trump rally. During the 1921 Tulsa race massacre, an eruption of violence turned into a two-day rampage in which white mobs targeted and destroyed black-owned businesses in an area known as Black Wall Street. As many as thirty-nine people were killed, most of them black.

Since George Floyd, a forty-six-year-old black man, had been killed by a white Minneapolis police officer in late May 2020, the country had been beset by violent protests, sometimes turning into riots, in cities nationwide. So, in addition to the Juneteenth rally date, Tulsa's history of racial violence was too much of an angle for the media to ignore.

Most of the campaign staffers I worked with felt that the president was once again being treated unfairly by a biased media who would not hold Democrats to the same strict standards. What was most offensive was that reporters were treating a Trump rally as something that was, on its face, a racist event that was wholly incompatible with anything involving black history, and they had decided that certain dates and places were simply not available to us. That virtually every news outlet began their stories with this premise was, to me, inescapable proof of their anti-Trump bias.

I believe this point was validated when the media had almost an identical reaction to the initial announcement that Trump would accept the nomination of the Republican Party in Jacksonville, Florida, in August 2020. Upon learning the date and location, the media breathlessly related the details of racial violence that had occurred there in 1960, when a crowd of white men beat black civil rights protesters with bats and ax handles. The implication was that Trump shouldn't be allowed to hold an event in that city either because it had been the location of the attack—known as "Ax Handle Saturday"—sixty years earlier.

Inside the campaign, we wondered if there were any city in America which the media would deem an acceptable location for a Trump event. To me, the behavior of the media on these points revealed them to be reflexively opposed to anything the president did. When Trump made an announcement, they were against it, and it was only a matter of figuring out why each time.

As it happened, the Jacksonville nomination never occurred because COVID-19 intervened again, and the RNC's convention was moved to mostly virtual, with Trump accepting the nomination in an event on the White House lawn.

Responding to the uproar over Juneteenth, however, the president tweeted that he had decided to move the rally date by one day:

> We had previously scheduled our #MAGA Rally in Tulsa, Oklahoma, for June 19th—a big deal. Unfortunately, however, this would fall on the Juneteenth Holiday. Many of my African American friends and supporters have reached out to suggest that we

consider changing the date out of respect for this Holiday, and in observance of this important occasion and all that it represents. I have therefore decided to move our rally to Saturday, June 20th, in order to honor their requests.

If anyone thought the president would get credit for changing the date of the rally, they were wrong. NBC even ran a column under the headline "Trump's Juneteenth Tulsa rally might have been a mistake—or a racist dog whistle," which argued that the president had wanted to disrespect the anniversary on purpose, which was pure nonsense.

In the days just before the event, the *Wall Street Journal* published an interview with the president in which he said that it had been a black Secret Service agent who had first alerted him to the significance of the date. Trump also told the paper, "I did something good; I made Juneteenth very famous." That was undeniably true, and I was certain that because Trump had planned a rally on June 19, millions of Americans were newly aware of what the Juneteenth holiday represents.

With the date of the rally reset, the opposition media changed tactics to begin describing the Tulsa rally in the most apocalyptic terms imaginable to convince people not to attend because of COVID-19.

USA Today reported that the rally stirred "fear of COVID-19 super spreader event." A *New York Times* headline warned that "Trump's Rally in Tulsa Could Spread Virus." *Business Insider* said that "Trump's Oklahoma rally is extremely risky." The negative headlines were endless and the hostile cable channels and legacy networks spent considerable air time warning their viewers to stay away from Tulsa.

Five days before the rally, campaign manager Brad Parscale tweeted that the event had more than a million ticket requests, which was a startling departure from how the campaign usually approached the public discussion of attendance figures. It was the general practice that no one put a number on the expected or actual attendance until the president himself did, because you didn't want to be the one who got contradicted. But as campaign manager, Brad was under pressure to deliver a perfect event, and pumping up excitement by releasing a big number was one way he decided to approach it.

That began a series of events that would plague the rally. Two days before show time, the Republican mayor of Tulsa, G. T. Bynum, declared a civil emergency in his city and announced a curfew for the area around the BOK Center, the event site.

"I have received information from the Tulsa Police Department and other law enforcement agencies that shows that individuals from organized groups who have been involved in destructive and violent behavior in other States are planning to travel to the city of Tulsa for purposes of causing unrest in and around the rally," the mayor said in an executive order that instituted the restrictions.

Anyone walking around Tulsa those few days could be forgiven for thinking they had stumbled into a futuristic urban war zone. Most businesses were boarded up as though they were Florida beach houses bracing for a hurricane, and there was tall, black steel fencing everywhere. Downtown Tulsa was fortified, and the fences standing eight or nine feet tall were intimidating reminders of a heavy law enforcement presence. National Guard troops had been activated to help provide security, and the groups of them standing guard or riding about in small utility vehicles lent a military air to the whole scene. During the daylight hours before the rally, Tulsa was a ghost town, and it served as a forewarning that our crowd might not be as large as we were expecting.

On Saturday morning, rally day, I did a hit with Michael Smerconish on CNN, standing on a scaffolding outside Tulsa's BOK Center, which held around nineteen thousand people. A picture taken of me during that appearance is the cover photograph for this book, in fact. In my remarks, I reminded viewers that President Trump would be making a separate speech at an outdoor stage where an anticipated overflow crowd would be gathered. Smerconish's questions were all about the virus, whether it was wise to allow so many people together in an indoor arena, and whether we were sacrificing health so that we could get the split-screen contrast of a rowdy Trump rally with a sleepy, socially distanced Biden event.

Later that morning, after I'd returned to the campaign's hotel headquarters, I got word that some members of the advance team had tested positive for the coronavirus. This was about the worst thing that could have happened at that point, because it was exactly what the media were looking for and there was zero chance that the information would not become public. In fact, just after I learned of the positive tests, I was notified by the White House comms shop that NBC News had asked about the issue. That meant that we had to issue a statement fast and just be done with it.

We announced that six staffers had tested positive, as detected by the hundreds of tests our traveling group had undergone since arriving in Tulsa. Some of the campaign workers had been on the ground for a week already, and I think we had to revise the number of positive tests upward to eight later in the morning.

"No COVID-positive staffers or anyone in immediate contact will be at today's rally or near attendees and elected officials," I told the media. The little wave of COVID-19 infections set off a blizzard of new stories about the dangers inherent in our campaign rally, and so I reiterated which precautions we were taking, saying that "all rally attendees are given temperature checks before going through security, at which point they are given wristbands, face masks, and hand sanitizer."

We pressed on because there was no chance at all that the rally would not proceed. But as the time approached, it was obvious that people were not turning out in great enough numbers to fill the arena, let alone require a second stage outside for an overflow crowd. Reports from the Secret Service on the total number of people going through the magnetometers gave an indication of the progress of arrivals, and it was significantly behind the pace that we would normally expect.

We canceled the planned outside remarks for both the president and vice president, though we didn't give a reason. Many media outlets broadcast the news of the cancelation and noted that social media pictures of the exterior of the BOK Center showed a sparse crowd at that time.

We understood that President Trump, still on the ground in DC, was livid about the coverage of the advance team's COVID-19 infections and that it was overshadowing the rally itself, which it certainly was. In the end, the Tulsa fire marshal reported that only 6,200 people were inside the BOK Center during the event, although we had a slightly higher number from the Secret Service. I saw the argument about the correct number as irrelevant, because even the higher total wouldn't have filled the place, and it certainly wouldn't have spilled out onto the nearby streets as an overflow crowd.

The president made an oblique reference to the disappointing turnout at the top of his speech, in a compliment to the people who did show up.

"I just want to thank all of you, you are warriors," he said. "I've been watching the fake news for weeks now, and everything is negative. Don't go, don't come, don't do anything. Today it was like, I've never seen anything like it. I've never seen anything like it. You are warriors, thank you."

After the speech, as we packed up to leave, I sought out Parscale because I had been manifested on Air Force One for the trip home. I figured that, with all the positive tests among staff, it was unlikely that I'd catch a ride.

"No campaign staff on the plane," Brad confirmed. "Trust me, you don't want to be on board tonight. You really don't."

I was sure that he was right. It didn't sound like a pleasant time with an angry and frustrated President Trump, and I wasn't terribly disappointed to be missing out.

Teenagers on TikTok and other social media sites claimed credit for the small crowd because they had bombarded our website with ticket requests, which they believed had kept the tickets out of the hands of real supporters. This actually wasn't possible, because there weren't any real tickets to Trump rallies. We asked that people sign up so that we could capture their cell phone number, but we issued no ticket or pass. So, even if TikTok kids had made a billion ticket requests, it wouldn't have mattered, but that didn't stop reporters from writing gleeful stories giving the kids credit anyway.

At one point, I was instructed to issue a statement that blamed the poor attendance on protesters outside the black steel fences, with a claim that they made it difficult for our supporters to get to the security gates to gain entry to the arena. But in truth, the problems with the Tulsa rally were many.

The publicity over the million ticket requests certainly hadn't helped, because it may have served to discourage people who didn't want to get immersed in such a huge crowd. The rumors of violent protests and the declaration of emergency by the mayor certainly deterred people from driving to Tulsa for a political event. The militarization and apparent evacuation of downtown Tulsa created the illusion that a great danger was approaching, which could easily scare off families that were usually common at Trump rallies. A week and a half of relentless cable television segments about the health threat posed by the rally probably convinced many people that it was too risky to attend. And perhaps Americans remained a little skittish about gathering in large crowds while people were still getting sick from the virus.

In sum, it was a complete and total disaster that could not have gone worse. Until it did.

Herman Cain, business leader and former Republican presidential candidate, was in Tulsa for the rally as a strong supporter and cochairman of the Black Voices for Trump voter coalition. Nine days later, he tested positive for COVID-19 in Georgia and went to the hospital two days after that. On July 30, 2020, he died from what were described as complications from COVID-19.

Immediately, the media pounced on the terrible news and blamed Cain's attendance at the Trump rally for his death. In effect, the media were saying that Donald Trump had killed Herman Cain, even though no one could prove where he had gotten infected.

Kayleigh McEnany addressed the issue from the White House briefing room, saying, "I will not politicize Herman Cain's passing, and I would just note the great contributions he's made to our society. We'll always remember him, and his legacy will stand."

Cain's friends and colleagues pointed out that he had been doing a lot of traveling around that time period and had also visited Arizona, which was experiencing a spike in cases. But none of that changed the fact that Cain was dead and left behind a wife, two adult children, and four grandchildren.

Not much time passed before it became clear that someone had to take the fall for the Tulsa catastrophe. Michael Glassner, the campaign's chief operating officer who specialized in planning and executing rallies for the president, was demoted and reassigned to handle ongoing legal affairs. I issued a statement to that effect, which denied that the move had anything to do with the failure of the rally:

> This is not a reaction to Tulsa. Michael Glassner is moving into the long-term role of navigating the many legal courses we face, including suits against major media outlets, some of which will likely extend beyond the end of the campaign. He is one of the founding members of Team Trump and his dedication to the success of the President is unmatched.

The enduring image of the Tulsa rally is the picture of President Trump returning from Oklahoma to the White House late that night. Trump emerged from Marine One, as the helicopter that carried him to the lawn of the White House is designated, looking tired and somewhat downcast. He still wore his blue suit, but his collar was open, and his trademark red tie was untied, hanging loosely around his neck. He carried a red Make America Great Again hat in his hand as he walked across the lawn, aware that the cameras were on him as they always were. He didn't approach the cameras to give any statements, and he offered only a quick wave and a thumbs up before he disappeared from view.

When MSNBC discussed the debacle in the days following the event, they rolled that tape of Trump returning home and accompanied it with a chyron that rubbed it in: "TEAM TRUMP BOASTED 1,000,000 REGISTERED FOR TULSA RALLY; ONLY 6,200 TURNED UP."

For once, they were hard to argue with.

The president's re-election was not lost that day in Tulsa, but it was a definite blow to the psyche of the campaign. There were still nearly five months to go until Election Day, there were still debates to come, and there would still be hundreds of millions of dollars spent on advertising. But in retrospect, I do think that Tulsa marked an undeniable turning point, even if we didn't know it at the time.

13

 ## An Intervention and Rehab
2007

My father's sister, Kathy Walton, came to Virginia in October 2007 and we made plans to go out to dinner. She had always been my favorite aunt and so I looked forward to it, although I was wary of being around her because of the consistently drunken state I was in. Aunt Kathy had quit drinking decades before and was extremely good at spotting people who were having problems.

Her son Brian (my cousin) and I met in her hotel room, and we all had a quick, superficial conversation at the beginning, so I could sense that something was awry. I looked around suspiciously but didn't see anything, until the door opened to reveal my father, mother, and brother walking into the room. There was another person with them, a woman whom I didn't know. Instantly, I knew exactly was going on— they were staging an intervention for me, and the woman was a paid interventionist.

Over the next several hours, they took turns telling me how much they loved me and were worried about me. They read letters written by cousins and friends who could not be present, including my cousin Joe, who I'd always been closest to, and implored me to go to an in-patient substance abuse facility they'd found in New Jersey.

One letter, from my oldest friend, Mike Fisher, was explicit about how he saw the problem: "Straight up, this is not a new issue. The drinking has gotten worse over the last few years, and I can whole-heartedly say, the wheels have fallen off," he wrote, saying that, while drunk, I am like a "high maintenance zombie reduced to a comatose state of staring into space while fighting for coherent thoughts."

Mike added that, "There is no need to recount the mental and physical escapades you go through when you reach this state, but I am saddened that you make the choice each day to start down that path."

After a long time in the room, I needed a cigarette, and Brian and I went down to the street level in front of the hotel to smoke. While we were there, I asked for his assessment of the situation.

"Until I agree to go to rehab, we're just going to sit in that room all night, aren't we?" I asked.

"That's how it looks," Brian said.

I nodded and crushed out my cigarette.

"Okay, let's go," I said.

Seabrook was a very nice addiction treatment center near Bridgeton, New Jersey, and the people there were understanding, kind, and professional. It was my first experience with rehab, and I was in a twenty-eight-day program. After ten days or so, I was feeling great. I had started to be more vocal in Alcoholics Anonymous meetings at Seabrook and I took part in a lot of the discussions in the classes we attended. As I neared the halfway point of my stay, my thoughts began to drift back to my employment situation.

Before I left, I had applied for the vacant position of press secretary in Virginia senator John Warner's office. I thought I had a decent chance of getting it because Warner, a Republican, was George Allen's mentor, and I hoped that I could get a recommendation for the job from Senator Allen.

Periodically, I was able to use a house phone to check my messages, and one day there was a message inviting me to come speak to Senator Warner about the position. My next call was to my father, and I told him that I wanted to sign myself out of the treatment program early.

"You're not ready," he said. "It's too soon."

I protested. "I feel great," I said. "If I don't take a chance at this job, I'm going to resent it, and it would affect the way I finish the twenty-eight days."

"If you do get the job, you'll just screw it up," he said.

I knew he was right, but I was desperate to get back into a job that I felt equaled my value, and I resented that my father was preventing me from taking a swing at it. I can see now that I have always pinned my identity to what I do for a living, and at that moment, I wanted to be Senator Warner's press secretary more than I wanted anything in the world.

My father relented and, with my mother's help, delivered my car to Seabrook within a couple of days. After signing myself out, "against medical advice," as they say, I got into my car and managed to get about an hour down the road before I stopped for my first drink.

I was hungover when I went to meet with Senator Warner a few days later. I spoke with him, and he got Senator Allen on the phone to do a sort of three-way interview, and then I went to the Senate chamber with his chief of staff to watch some of the floor activity. We had a nice conversation, and I wondered throughout if I smelled of alcohol.

Soon, I was informed that the senator wanted to offer the job to someone who was earlier in their career than I was, because it wasn't fair to offer someone like me a job that was essentially temporary. It was cast as a favor to me that they were offering the job to someone else.

At the time, I think I took that at face value because I needed to believe it was true so I could avoid taking responsibility for sinking my chances myself. It seems so obvious now that they probably just didn't have faith that I could do the job and stay sober, but simply didn't want to say that.

The result of all that was that I had bailed out on rehab, was still jobless, and was drinking more than ever. It was the drunk trifecta.

14

Parscale Out, Stepien In
June and July 2020

The aftershocks from the Tulsa rally continued into the next month.

It was not unusual for me to be approached by reporters who had heard rumors that Brad Parscale was about to be fired from his job as campaign manager for President Trump. We had been hearing different theories or versions of his dismissal for months, dating to well before that fateful rally in Oklahoma.

Parscale was a significant political celebrity, which everyone understood to annoy the president from time to time, and there was always speculation that Trump believed that Brad was making too much money off the campaign. I had no idea what his financial arrangements were, but I do know that Brad was extremely recognizable in public, as I personally experienced on several occasions when I walked through crowded airports with him. His six-foot-eight stature, barrel chest, bushy beard, and spiky reddish hair certainly set him apart from most people.

And he surely didn't shun the spotlight. Since I had joined the campaign in February 2019, there had been many profiles written about

Parscale in various national publications, and he had done a good amount of television, including some of the network morning shows and *60 Minutes*.

In January 2020, I accompanied Brad for two days of media appearances in New York City. One of his TV interviews was with the morning show on CBS, and we arrived to discover that we were sharing the green room with legendary actor Patrick Stewart, who was there to promote a new *Star Trek* series called *Picard*.

As a lifelong *Star Trek* fan, it was a thrill for me to be in the presence of Captain Jean-Luc Picard, so without thinking I pulled out my phone to take some pictures of Brad and Sir Patrick chatting. Stewart's assistant rushed over to order me to stop, so I only managed to take a couple of shots before I put the phone away. It struck me as odd that Stewart and his assistant were jumpy about pictures being taken, since he was about to go on national television anyway. But after some thought, I concluded that their objection wasn't to the picture itself, but that being photographed with the head of the Trump campaign was the problem.

In some media cases, I spent a lot of time on the phone with adversarial journalists who were writing profiles that were highly critical of Brad. We fought off as many attack pieces as we could, because negative stories about the campaign certainly didn't help the president get re-elected. And for a while it seemed like attacking Brad was the media's method of keeping us occupied and distracted from the real work of running the campaign.

After Tulsa, the questions about Parscale's job security increased dramatically, with reporters reaching out daily to try to substantiate fresh gossip, or to bounce theoretical questions off me.

In a *Washington Post* story that hit on the afternoon of July 12, 2020, reporters Michael Scherer and Josh Dawsey put together a pretty accurate account of the moods and machinations that were evident inside the White House and the campaign.

"Trump has made clear his displeasure with Parscale, especially after a disappointing rally in Tulsa, and the campaign has expanded its senior team in ways that diminish his role," the *Post* reported, citing Jared Kushner, Bill Stepien, Jason Miller, and Hope Hicks among those who had either new or expanded roles in campaign leadership.

The next day, CNN ran a story on its website under the headline, "Amid rising coronavirus cases, the Trump campaign struggles to get its rally machine going." It referenced the Tulsa rally, as well as one in New Hampshire that we had canceled because of potential bad weather, although it had cleared up by the time the event would have started. Also included in the CNN piece was a healthy dose of general and anonymous disgruntlement with how the campaign was going.

"I think there is a growing sense of concern that the campaign isn't functioning as we want it to," one unnamed Trump donor told CNN. Elsewhere in the story, the same person was quoted again: "I think Parscale probably needs to go. I think a lot of folks would feel more comfortable with someone who's actually run a campaign before."

Two days after that, President Trump demoted Parscale and replaced him with Stepien. The public announcement came in a Facebook post and then on Twitter.

I am pleased to announce that Bill Stepien has been promoted to the role of Trump Campaign Manager. Brad Parscale, who has been with me for a very long time and has led our tremendous digital and data strategies, will remain in that role, while being a Senior Advisor to the campaign. Both were heavily involved in our historic 2016 win, and I look forward to having a big and very important second win together. This one should be a lot easier as our poll numbers are rising fast, the economy is getting better, vaccines and therapeutics will soon be on the way, and Americans want safe streets and communities!

The announcement made big news in the political world, with headlines springing up on websites around the globe. And, in what I thought was an unusual move, but probably helpful, Brad showed up at the campaign headquarters the next morning to speak to the staff and formally hand over the reins to Stepien.

Portions of Parscale's remarks were extremely emotional as he thanked the staff for their work during his tenure. He said that he had devoted five years of his life to the Trump family, and that he was not going to go too far away in his new role as an advisor on digital and data issues. He also had praise for Stepien, calling him a talented political mind. Stepien accepted the handoff and thanked Parscale for leading the campaign to that point. Justin Clark became the new deputy campaign manager.

With less than four months to go before the election, the president's campaign had a new leadership team. Stepien's personality and approach were certainly different from Parscale's. Stepien was quieter, gruff at times, and, I thought, difficult to read, whereas Parscale had been louder and more gregarious. Stepien seemed to be more organized, while Parscale appeared to flow with the current of the campaign.

Logistically, Stepien made two changes that affected our routines. He instituted daily 8 a.m. senior staff meetings, which we had not held up to that point, and he began to have frequent all-staff meetings, where all departments would give updates and all employees could hear from the campaign's leaders.

I welcomed the daily morning meetings, because they established some order to the beginning of each campaign day that had been lacking before. They did, however, make fitting in my morning runs

Tim Murtaugh, age two, with his grandfather, Danny Murtaugh of the Pittsburgh Pirates, in 1971.

Young Tim Murtaugh with his parents, Janet and Tim Murtaugh, at Three Rivers Stadium in Pittsburgh, circa 1971.

Tim Murtaugh (left) with longtime friend Mike Fisher around Halloween, circa 1976.

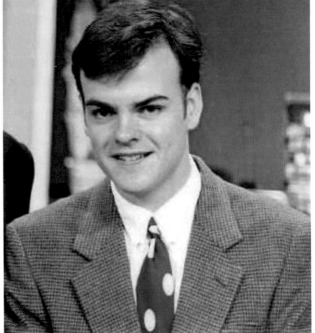

Tim Murtaugh as an anchor on a student television broadcast at Temple University, circa 1990.

Tim Murtaugh in the booth at WBQB/WFVA radio in Fredericksburg, VA, in the early 1990s.

Tim Murtaugh and Dena Kozanas with their dog, Ollie, upon the completion of canine obedience class in 2011.

Tim Murtaugh and Dena Kozanas on their wedding day, August 17, 2014.

Tim Murtaugh (right) with parents, Tim and Janet Murtaugh, and brother, Steve Murtaugh, in Florida for baseball spring training, March 2015.

Tim Murtaugh with Rep. Lou Barletta, June 2016.

Tim Murtaugh and Agriculture Secretary Sonny Perdue, about to board a seaplane in Alaska, July 2018.

Tim Murtaugh with Brad Parscale on the rooftop deck at campaign HQ in Rosslyn, June 12, 2019.

Older brother meets baby brother, September 2018.

Left: Tim Murtaugh with Democratic candidate for president Beto O'Rourke at WFAA-TV in Dallas, October 17, 2019.

Below: Aboard Air Force One with Brad Parscale (left), November 2019.

Name card on Air Force One, autographed by the boss.

Backstage at the rally in Battle Creek, Michigan on December 18, 2019, the same night as the first impeachment votes.

Hogan Gidley, White House principal deputy press secretary takes a picture of his handiwork, a sign to communicate to Trump the results of the impeachment vote, back stage at a rally in Battle Creek, Michigan, December 18, 2019.

Kayleigh McEnany holding a sign to communicate to President Trump on stage about the impeachment vote that had just happened, December 18, 2019.

Vice President Mike Pence watches the impeachment proceedings on Fox News while President Trump speaks on stage in Battle Creek, Michigan on December 18, 2019.

Security barriers on the streets of Tulsa before the rally on June 20, 2020.

President Trump and First Lady Melania Trump greet the staff immediately after the first presidential debate in Cleveland, September 29, 2020.

On set with Bill Hemmer on Fox News at the site of the first presidential debate in Cleveland, September 28, 2020.

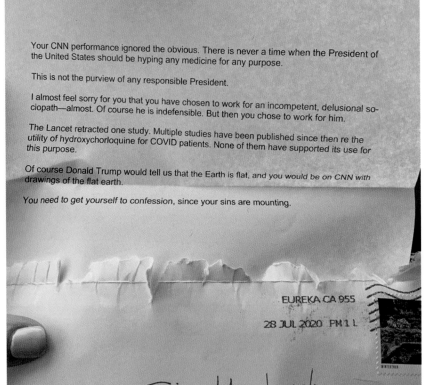

Your CNN performance ignored the obvious. There is never a time when the President of the United States should be hyping any medicine for any purpose.

This is not the purview of any responsible President.

I almost feel sorry for you that you have chosen to work for an incompetent, delusional sociopath—almost. Of course he is indefensible. But then you chose to work for him.

The Lancet retracted one study. Multiple studies have been published since then re the utility of hydroxychlorloquine for COVID patients. None of them have supported its use for this purpose.

Of course Donald Trump would tell us that the Earth is flat, and you would be on CNN with drawings of the flat earth.

You need to get yourself to confession, since your sins are mounting.

EUREKA CA 955

28 JUL 2020 PM 1 L

Tim Murtaugh

Hate mail, July 2020.

September 17, 2020

Tim Murtaugh, Communications Director,
Trump 2020 Campaign,
1300 N. 17th Street, 14th Floor,
Arlington, Virginia
22209

Mr. Murtaugh:

I watched a part of your appearance on CNN last night. The grim expression on your face
suggested you might be constipated which lines up with what you were saying. You're full of
shit, but why would I expect otherwise from a **Donald Trump** supporter.

A global perspective says Mr. Trump is a dangerous idiot, a domestic terrorist, an international
thug, a Russian stooge, and a failed businessman who wouldn't know truth if it fucked him up
the ass dry. And, oh yes, he is personally responsible for the deaths of tens of thousands of
Americans. That's only a start.

Odd though that there are people in the United States like you, large numbers of people who
appear to be saying enthusiastically that, "Hey, this is the kind of person we want in the White
House!"

Where in hell is your moral compass?

Yours truly,

Hate mail, September 2020.

Waiting for a TV hit alongside John Roberts of Fox News the day before the final debate, Nashville, October 21, 2020.

With President Trump backstage at the Nashville debate, October 22, 2020.

Last chance TV hits on Election Day, November 3, 2020

President Trump speaks to the press at his campaign headquarters in Rosslyn, Virginia on Election Day, November 3, 2020.

Election Night, actually 1:58 a.m. on November 4, 2020

more difficult and it looked like I wouldn't reach my goal of becoming one of those rare people who finish a campaign in better physical condition than when it began.

While I didn't have access to the campaign's overall planning documents, it became immediately clear that Stepien and Clark were concerned about the campaign's finances. When the campaign began to reduce the amount of television time it had reserved for advertising in key states in the fall, we had to beat back the perception that we were running short on money, even though that was getting close to being true.

I remember one particularly heated conversation with a reporter from Reuters, who was insisting on writing a story about our reduced advertising outlays. I asked for an assist from Kaelan Dorr, who did a lot with our paid media buys, and together we yelled at the reporter for about five minutes. Predictably, it didn't do any good, and that story, like others, helped to paint an emerging picture of a campaign in trouble.

 My First DUI
2008

For the last thirteen months of President George W. Bush's second term, I served as a political appointee in the Pension Benefit Guaranty Corporation, a little-known quasi-independent agency that insures private pension funds. I managed to work there for more than a year without learning a blessed thing about insuring private pension funds.

I don't know if any of my coworkers ever caught on, but I often disappeared for hours, which was when I would go to bars that were far enough away to guarantee that I wouldn't see any coworkers. Some days, if I felt too hungover to contemplate drinking, I'd drive home as quickly as possible and grab a quick nap. Other times I would try to sleep in brief stretches in my car parked at the office, but I tried to avoid that as a frequent practice because I thought it was too risky.

After being an enormous pain in the ass to my cousin Brian, sleeping on his couch for far too long during a time of separation from my then wife, Tayne Renmark, I had finally gotten my own place in Arlington County, and became a regular at the three-story Crystal City

Sports Pub. I went there every day, and on weekends I might put in three separate shifts at the bar. In the morning, I might walk over for breakfast screwdrivers, to be followed by a late-morning nap and then a liquid lunch at the bar for round two. By happy hour I'd be ready for the serious drinking that came when the sun went down.

Aside from rent, car insurance, and gasoline, nearly every penny I made was spent at the Sports Pub. I was making $130,000 a year as a GS-15 Schedule C appointee in the federal government, but I was nearly broke all the time. I actually made calculations, dividing the cash I had left in my checking account by the number of days left before pay day, so that I could determine how much I could spend at the bar each night.

My entire existence was built around sitting at the bar and getting loaded. Getting up and going to work, pretending to understand what I was doing while I was there—those were just the motions I had to go through to receive the money I needed to keep drinking.

In July 2008, I was at home one day and got a call from a friend inviting me down to Richmond. I was already good and loaded when he called, and in the hour or so before I got in the car, I drank some more.

While I was driving in stop-and-go traffic on the highway, I was foolishly checking my email on my work phone and failed to notice that the car in front of me had come to a stop. I rear-ended it at a very low speed, but hard enough to make us both pull over to the shoulder to exchange information. There was no real damage to either vehicle, but as we stood and discussed the situation, a Virginia State Trooper appeared on the scene and began to file a report. It wasn't long before he had me doing field sobriety tests, and then a breathalyzer, and the next thing I knew I was in handcuffs in the back seat of his cruiser.

This was my first real trouble with the law as a direct result of my drinking, and I wasn't terribly sure what it all meant. I can remember being transported to a State Police field station of some kind, where one of my handcuff bracelets was removed from my wrist and clasped to a metal rail bolted to a wall. I tried to appeal to the female trooper on duty.

"Do I look like a flight risk?" I asked, although she didn't find me amusing.

I was convicted of driving under the influence, and my blood alcohol level had been high enough that it warranted a mandatory five-day stretch in jail, according to Virginia law. I took vacation time from work to report to the lockup to serve my sentence, didn't tell anyone about it, and got severely drunk the night before I was to turn myself in.

I spent the five days in extreme discomfort with an ailment that I likely misdiagnosed myself. What I wrote off as an extended hangover following my pre-jail binge was probably actually withdrawal. I have since learned that alcohol withdrawal is one of the more dangerous situations any addict can be in—it can cause seizures and even be fatal.

When I had finished my little hitch in jail, I didn't waste any time going right back to drinking. Nothing had really changed, except that my driver's license was suspended for a year. I could have gotten one of those ignition interlock devices installed, but I decided that was a bad look, so I passed on that and just didn't drive.

All in all, the DUI conviction was barely a speed bump for me and changed nothing.

I ran out the clock in the Bush 43 administration, and was sitting at the bar at the Sports Pub at noon on Tuesday, January 20, 2009, when Barack Obama was sworn in. I took a shot of Jägermeister when Obama said, "So help me, God" at the end of his oath, and I was unemployed once again.

One night walking home from the Sports Pub, I had thought that someone was following me, and for some reason I turned and threw my keys in the direction of the nonexistent assailant. In the dark, I couldn't find the keys in some bushes where I thought they might have landed, and I suddenly found myself with no way to get into my apartment.

I was able to wake one of my Sports Pub cronies who lived in the neighborhood and crash on the couch, but the next day I still couldn't find my keys. It was easy enough to get a copy of the apartment key from my landlord, but the car key was a different problem. Even though I wasn't a licensed driver at the moment, it still seemed like a good idea to have a key to the car anyway.

I owned a Saab, which apparently presented a serious problem in my situation. The key was actually an oversized fob that contained a chip in the tapered end. When you inserted it into the little notch in the center panel between the two front seats, the chip communicated with the ignition system and allowed you to start the car. Without the key and the chip, it was impossible to make a copy. As a result, the whole central panel and ignition port needed to be replaced, and it cost me almost $3,000.

That one night had turned out to be a wildly expensive trip to the pub.

Another time, I had planned to catch a train to meet my brother Steve at Madison Square Garden to see our shared favorite band, Rush. I intended to go—really, I did—but as the day approached it seemed like such an enormous task for someone who frequently sat for days in drunk hermit mode. The day of the show I told him that I was not going to make it, and my mother later told me that he was extremely let down.

It was still early in 2009 when I got a call from my old pal Tucker Martin, with whom I'd last worked on the Kilgore campaign for governor of Virginia in 2005. Since that election, he'd been working for Bob McDonnell, who'd been elected attorney general on the same day that Kilgore lost the governor's race, and now McDonnell was preparing to run for governor himself.

Martin had the idea to plant me at the state party—RPV again—to be the "bomb thrower" in the media so that the McDonnell campaign could stay on a positive message of what he wanted to do for the people of the Commonwealth. It sounded like a pretty good idea and I happily agreed.

RPV was still located on Grace Street in downtown Richmond when I arrived for my second tour of duty ten years after my first, this time to help Bob McDonnell get elected governor. There was a tiny parking lot in the back, accessible by an alley, where I stashed my car because, without a license, I didn't plan to drive it except in emergencies.

Day drinking was still very much a thing for me, and I reacquainted myself with the Penny Lane Pub, which had changed locations a few blocks closer to where RPV was. Most days I would walk over at lunch time, have a series of beers and Liverpool Kisses, and order a shepherd's pie to go. I got drunk enough in that time frame to carry me through the afternoon, and I would find my way back to the Pub again after 5 p.m.

In July 2009, I celebrated my fortieth birthday by spending the weekend at the high-end Jefferson Hotel in Richmond. That Saturday I made a presentation to a Republican organization that promoted leadership opportunities for women in politics. Dena Kozanas was in that group, and I think it was the first time I'd spoken to her since the Thelma Drake race in 2006. It was good to see her again.

McDonnell turned out to be a fantastic candidate, our Democratic opponent was awful, and we won by more than seventeen points. Though I was drinking heavily the whole time through the campaign and the entire year is mostly a blur, I thought I probably had repaired my overall reputation for a little while.

That belief was reinforced when I got a phone call from the Republican Governors Association (RGA), with which we'd worked during the campaign. The RGA had a big election year coming up in 2010, with thirty-seven governor's races around the country, and was staffing up for the cycle. I traveled to DC to meet with political director Paul Bennecke and executive director Nick Ayers. After a brief interview process, they offered me a job, and I started as the director of political communications at the beginning of 2010.

The job at the RGA was a lot of fun. We ran a lot of air campaigns, meaning we placed a lot of television ads in states that had competitive governor's races. The ads were sometimes supported by attack websites, as we targeted opponents with negative ads as a general tactic. It was political carpet bombing, and it was a blast.

I had much professional respect for Ayers and Bennecke, who were two Georgia guys who had risen to prominence and were associated with Sonny Perdue. But as had happened in other positions, my behavior failed to show them or the job the respect that they deserved.

I again got an apartment in Crystal City to be close to the Sports Pub, because even though I had my driver's license back, I wanted to avoid driving as much as possible. But that winter, on a day when there was a ton of snow on the ground, a fellow RGA employee asked me for a ride into the office. I recognized a drinking opportunity when I heard one, so I told him that if he met me at the Sports Pub, we could ride in together. This was an occasion when the Sports Pub's 7 a.m. opening time would come in handy.

I made sure to be at the Sports Pub a few minutes after it opened the doors, because I felt it would be conspicuous and embarrassing to be waiting on the sidewalk for the bartender to come unlock the place. Once seated at the bar, I started out with screwdrivers and played with my phone while I got a morning buzz going. I had not yet gone into work at the RGA while newly intoxicated—hungover, yes, but not riding a new drunk.

About twenty minutes before my coworker was to appear, I switched to Irish coffee, which seemed like a good idea at the time.

I was thinking that having a coffee drink in front of me might fool someone into believing that no alcohol was involved.

My coworker showed up and we went off to work, arriving at the RGA offices on time and without incident. I was pretty buzzed and I stayed at my desk, trying to concentrate on a press release I was writing while avoiding interactions with anyone else.

About mid-morning, Nick Ayers showed up at the door and nodded his head at me.

"Can I talk to you for a minute?" he asked quietly.

I followed him to his office, and he shut the door and sat down, gesturing for me to join him in a small sitting area in front of his desk.

"What's going on today?" Ayers asked me.

I shook my head and gestured with my hands to convey confusion at the question. "What do you mean?" I asked.

"I mean, I think you've been drinking," he said.

I dropped the pretense that I was sober and accepted his offer of a ride home. In the car, Ayers asked me to take a couple of days to reflect, refresh, and recharge, and return to work the following week with a new approach. I thanked him sincerely for understanding and for giving me a second chance, and then I proceeded to get drunk and stay drunk until I passed out late Sunday night.

I went to work on Monday, and I did manage to keep things between the lines for a few months. Though I was constantly hungover, I didn't drink before or during work hours for a good long while, which counted as a victory for me.

I had begun spending time with Dena Kozanas, so I had more to look forward to some nights after work than just sitting at the bar all alone. Dena said she was interested in starting her own business advising candidates on compliance with fundraising law and other federal campaign requirements, which I thought was a good model for a business because every campaign needs advice like that. Our meetings began at her request, because she said she wanted to pick my brain to identify potential clients.

Naturally I asked her to meet me at the Sports Pub, where we sat at one of the upstairs bars where I could still snoke cigarettes. We would sit and talk about people we both knew in Virginia political circles, and I tried to get her to drink on my pace. I even got her to do a kamikaze shot, I think. Looking back, I am amazed that Dena ever agreed to meet me like that more than once, but we did do that several times.

Then I asked her out for what I regarded as our first real date, involving entering the Sports Pub's bar Olympics competition, in which co-ed teams competed in darts, pool, beer pong, and other drinking-friendly games. I suggested that we meet one Sunday at the Sports Pub to "practice" the events so we would be ready for the real competition the following week. How romantic is that?

When we met on Sunday, it was obvious right away that we wouldn't be able to engage in a lot of the bar games because the pool tables were covered up and there was a larger-than-usual crowd on hand. After a minute, I figured out that it was the day of the gold medal game—USA versus Canada—in men's hockey at the Winter Olympics. We stayed and watched the game anyway, which must have been a scintillating first date for Dena, who couldn't care less about most sports. We went on better dates after that, but I never did anything to alter how much I was drinking. I just made a stronger effort to conceal it.

At work at the RGA, things stayed reasonably stable for a while until one day in August, when I woke up early one weekday and just started drinking. Simple as that, I grabbed a bottle and started boozing before I got in the shower to get ready for work. I don't know why; I just woke up and did it.

By the time I got to work I was pretty drunk, and I don't remember the sequence of events at all. I just remember being put into a taxicab to be ferried home—no personal ride from Nick Ayers on that occasion—and when I "came to" at home many hours later, I sensed that I had crossed a line that was potentially professionally fatal. I inherently knew that while I had been shown compassion when I first turned up intoxicated on the job, it was not likely to happen a second time.

Indeed, when I returned to the office, I was summoned by Paul Bennecke.

"We're going to have to let you go," he said.

I asked him to give me another chance, which I knew was an unreasonable request from someone who had shown up for work hammered twice. And as a Hail Mary pass, I asked to be allowed to go to rehab and return once I had dried out.

"We don't have time for that," Bennecke said. "It's almost Labor Day in an election year. I'm sorry."

And just like that, I thought my career might be over. You don't get fired for being a degenerate alcoholic and come back from that very easily.

Dena could have understandably ditched me on the spot, but for some reason she didn't. She communicated with my family, helped me to get my affairs in order as best she possibly could, and supported me as I talked about going into an in-patient treatment facility again.

16

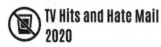 TV Hits and Hate Mail 2020

Since I had a background in television, doing the TV hits in my role as communications director for Trump wasn't a big deal. It had been years since I'd sat in front of a camera with regularity, but I figured it couldn't be too hard to get back into shape.

In the early months of 2019, there wasn't as much demand for representatives of the campaign as there would be later on, and Kayleigh McEnany handled most of the requests that did come in. I did do a few TV hits without meeting with disaster, and I felt like I found my footing pretty quickly. At first, I stayed in the comfort zone of Fox News, Newsmax, and some of the smaller, more partisan outlets like One America News Network (OANN). But eventually as time went on, I mixed in more challenging appearances on the "opposition" outlets like CNN, MSNBC, and some of the legacy broadcast networks.

My approach was simple. I tried to have an idea in my head of what the likely questions would be, what my answers should include, and which issues might come up that weren't related to our primary topic of discussion. Once I had those thoughts organized, I would boil down my strategy for an upcoming hit by answering a simple question for myself: What was I trying to accomplish in those four to six minutes on television?

Identifying what I wanted to say, rather than what the host wanted to talk about, was the key. Once that message was established in my head, I would mentally create a list of three things that I wanted to make sure I said while I was on the air.

The message depended on the situation, of course. While the Democratic primaries were still going on and numerous candidates were still in the race, sometimes we'd want to amplify their attacks on each other. Other times we'd want to talk about accomplishments of the Trump administration or highlight the booming economy. Once Joe Biden became the Democrats' nominee, we spent a lot of energy attacking him.

With most shows, certainly on Fox News and Newsmax, but even the ones on CNN and MSNBC, the producers would give us a decent idea of what they wanted to talk about. The friendlier the show was, the more information you'd tend to get in advance, but I don't recall ever being denied at least a hint of where the interviewer planned to take the conversation.

I found that speaking to local television outlets was often more challenging than typical quick hits on national outlets. The locals seemed to be less concerned with the horse race aspect of the election than the cable channels, which had to fill hours and hours of news time each day. Sometimes their questions were very local in nature, which sometimes meant I just had to say I wasn't familiar with the topic. Other times they came up with questions we hadn't heard or anticipated before.

One morning when we were in Dallas for a rally in October 2019, I was booked to do a live interview on the morning show at WFAA-TV, the local ABC affiliate. It was tremendously early, and the interview location was up on the roof of the affiliate's downtown building. It was cool that morning, and I was in position on the rooftop by 5:30 a.m.

The host asked me about President Trump's decision to withdraw American troops from Syria, a decision that had come under fire from lawmakers of both parties. Naturally, I was no expert in global military strategy or operations, nor was I a spokesman for the White House or Department of Defense, but it was live television and there had to be a response.

This wasn't a question that should be feared, but I use it here as an example, because the answer followed a simple three-step progression:

1. The president promised he was going to do this.
2. Now he's doing what he promised.
3. He was right to do it.

When you're speaking for the incumbent president running for re-election, this method of answering questions is a good one to commit to memory because you will use it a lot.

This interview sticks out among the many because of the guy I bumped into after I climbed back down to the newsroom from the roof. Booked to follow me on the WFAA morning show was none other than Beto O'Rourke, the former congressman from Texas who was, as of that day, still in the race for the Democratic Party's nomination for president. He was in the newsroom drinking a cup of coffee waiting for his turn on the air.

I walked over to him and introduced myself.

"Hey, Beto," I said, extending my hand. "I'm Tim Murtaugh. I'm the communications director for the Trump campaign."

"Oh, hey!" he said, and we shook hands while his staffer, a young woman, looked annoyed.

"What brings you to town?" I asked him, since he was from El Paso, over six hundred miles away.

"Oh, you know, campaign stuff," he said. "You're here for the Trump rally, obviously."

"Yeah," I said. "Hey, can I grab a picture with you?"

He happily agreed and I handed my phone to his staffer so she could take the picture. She was well beyond horrified by then.

I thanked him and we parted ways, but he had struck me as a pretty decent guy who didn't take every moment of the campaign as deadly serious. I can't stand his politics and I think he is a really bad candidate on whom Democratic donors have wasted a lot of money. But on that early morning in Dallas, he seemed like a nice fellow. He would drop out of the race just two weeks later, for lack of support and fundraising, on November 1, 2019.

On local hits like that one in Dallas, there was no possibility that President Trump would be watching, but if I appeared on Fox News, there was a decent chance that he'd see it, either live or when someone played it back for him. He was always interested in what his people were saying on television during the course of any day, and it took a little while before I realized just how closely he paid attention.

One day, just as I had gotten done with a Fox hit, my cell phone rang as I walked back to my desk. Looking at the screen, I saw only four zeros—0000—as the incoming number, which was unusual. I would normally ignore a number I didn't know, but something told me to take this call because I had a suspicion that I knew who it was.

"This is Tim," I said upon answering.

"Mr. Murtaugh?" said a female voice on the other end. "Do you have a moment to speak with the president?"

"Of course," I said. I mean, you can't really say no, right?

"Please hold," she said. And there was silence for a moment before a very familiar voice came on the line.

"Tim," said the president. "Just saw you on Fox News, great hit, you're doing a great job. Really great. Just one thing, the way we're talking about certain things needs to change a little bit."

And then he gave instructions on how he wanted certain topics discussed, which specific words he liked to use, and ways he thought we could lead public opinion in the direction he wanted. Perhaps this would not be a surprise to many people who have studied Donald J. Trump, as he was heavily interested in communication, in marketing, and he took the time to involve himself in calling the shots. The conversation went on for more than five minutes, with him doing almost all the talking.

He didn't call me after every hit—far from it—but it happened often enough that it wasn't a surprise anymore when it did. It added a layer of tension to Fox News television interviews, because in the back of my mind I knew there was a decent possibility that the president was watching and would call if he saw something he didn't think was quite right. But that was okay, because there are not many things cooler than being in a conversation with someone, looking down at your phone, and saying, "Oh, I have to take this. The president is calling."

There was a lower probability that President Trump would be watching CNN, MSNBC, or any of the legacy networks, but those hits came with different things to worry about. Alexa Henning, who had come over from the White House and ran our booking, or strategic communications, operation, would occasionally appear at my office door with a half-smile on her face.

I'd look up and see her standing there and know immediately what she wanted.

"What?" I'd ask.

"How do you feel about doing [insert hostile news show here]?" she'd ask.

"Ugh," I'd say. "What do they want to talk about?"

And she would run down the list of topics, and I would agree, because that's what we did, and then I'd dread the upcoming unpleasant TV hit until it happened. I really hated it when Alexa would drop by in the morning to ask about a prime-time show, because it meant that I had to think about it all day.

During the heavy COVID-19 months of 2020, when almost all the coverage of the campaign focused on the pandemic, I appeared twice on CNN with Brianna Keilar as the host. I think it would be accurate to conclude that Keilar had decided that she didn't like me before I ever appeared on her show.

In a June interview, Keilar pressed me about President Trump's remark that he had asked government officials to slow down testing for the coronavirus during the pandemic. Taking my lead from spokespeople at the White House, who had already described the remarks as a joke meant to illustrate a point, I was prepared for the question.

Keilar asked if it were true that the president wanted to slow down the pace of testing, even though more than one hundred thousand Americans had already died at that point.

"No, it's not," I said. "I understand there's not much of a sense of humor at CNN center, but the president was joking. He tried to illustrate the point that when you expand testing, you will naturally expand the number of positive cases that you detect."

"I'm not surprised that you're either unable or unwilling to understand the president had a tongue-in-cheek remark there," I continued. "But that's the point he's making."

Keilar decided that she would claim moral superiority and declare humor off limits, while dishonestly suggesting that the president and his campaign were laughing at the people who were dying of COVID-19.

She noted that 120,000 Americans had died in the pandemic so far, and added, "I do not think that is funny. Do you think that is funny?"

When I referred to the president's remarks as "ironic humor," she returned to her rhetorical indignation.

"Is dead Americans, is unemployed Americans, is that funny to you?" she demanded.

By the end of it, I had been unable to come up with a better retort than to insist that the president had been trying to use a joke to illustrate a point, and I had to repeat it several times. It was not my best performance, and a handful of left-leaning websites wrote gleeful stories about how she had "eviscerated" me during the segment. The whole thing was a reminder that I needed to anticipate their partisanship more and treat them as though they were the political opposition, because they clearly were.

In a related development a couple of days later, President Trump was asked by a reporter if he had indeed been joking when he said he'd told staff to slow down COVID-19 testing.

"I don't kid, let me just tell you. Let me make it clear," he said, denying that there had been any attempt at using humor to prove a point. He went on to make an argument against increasing testing because "by having more tests, we have more cases."

That wasn't far off the point we had said he was trying to make, but the fact that he said he wasn't joking sounded like he was contradicting us. This was a hazard you got accustomed to when working for Trump—when you went on the record about something, you couldn't be sure that the president wouldn't soon say exactly the opposite. That phenomenon, incidentally, was part of the reason why we had a campaign communications policy of never interpreting or explaining Trump's tweets. We always told reporters that the tweets spoke for themselves, and only the president could explain them, if he wanted to.

When I appeared again on Brianna Keilar's show a month later, I was better equipped to do battle with her, and again the prevalent topic was the coronavirus and issues like mask wearing and the US testing program. In one exchange, she revealed herself to be a partisan whose only interest in conducting an interview was to win an argument with the Trump campaign. And she was not above moving the goalposts to do it.

I argued that what Trump had achieved on coronavirus testing was remarkable, since prior to the outbreak of the pandemic, a test for this particular virus did not exist at all.

I began, "The testing program that the president has instituted here in this country, we tested—"

"What testing program?" Keilar interrupted.

"There was no test for the coronavirus because, prior to this, there was no coronavirus," I explained. "The test had to be invented first before it could be mass produced and spread around the country. And that's what the president has achieved. And 46 million tests have been conducted in this country. We're now testing 800,000 people a day."

And then the goalposts shifted. She dropped the argument that there was no testing program at all, and instead complained that the tests were too slow.

"They take two weeks and sometimes longer," Keilar said. "And you know that if you don't get the results back within five days, those tests are pointless. This is a testing failure, Tim."

"No, it is not," I said. "It's a tremendous success story. We're leading the world in testing. And 46 million tests of Americans and 800,000 tests a day."

And then she decided that she didn't like that measurement of testing and wanted to use a different metric instead.

"Not per capita, Tim," she said.

Frustration mounting, I continued. "It wasn't as though there was a coronavirus test sitting on the shelf somewhere that had to simply be mass produced. No. This test had to be invented in the first place.

That's why it's called a novel coronavirus. It's because no one had ever seen it before."

"Tim, I can't even," Keilar said. "There was a lot of stuff, swabs for the nose that didn't have to be like a wheel that had to be reinvented. You know that. And there were major problems getting those tests out. And you know that."

So, basically, her argument was:

1. There was no COVID-19 testing program.
2. Okay, there was a testing program, but it was too slow.
3. Okay, sure, the US led the world in total tests administered, but it wasn't good enough because we didn't also lead in per capita measurements.
4. Trump shouldn't get credit for the development of the tests because cotton swabs already existed.

This is what CNN put up during the daytime and presented as actual journalism.

But then our conversation shifted to President Trump's televised coronavirus briefings from the White House, including one that was upcoming.

"We're eagerly awaiting this coronavirus briefing the president is going to have," she said. "As far as we can tell, there won't be any experts there. So, what's the point of this?"

"I don't know who is going to be at the briefing or not," I said, because the coronavirus briefings were planned and controlled by the White House. "I would note when the president was having the briefing, largely the media was arguing that he should stop doing them. Then there was a period of time where he wasn't doing them, and the media began to complain about that."

"Okay, well, that's because—" Keilar began to respond before I interrupted her.

"And then not having even held the next one, you are already complaining about it, and it hasn't even happened yet," I said.

As we headed into the homestretch of the interview, it only got more heated when I brought up the alternative COVID-19 treatment of hydroxychloroquine and how the media had risen up against even discussing its possible benefit. Keilar went after it in slightly starker terms than even some of her colleagues might have done.

"It kills people," she said, and then, after little sparring, she really got rolling.

"If you're on here talking about hydroxychloroquine, I think you're doing a real disservice to the health of Americans," Keilar said. "I mean, if you're going to come on here and talk about how this is a good treatment, when doctors have said, no, it is not, and studies has been canceled because—"

"Dr. Fauci himself has said he would prescribe it," I interrupted again, name-checking the media's most blessed hero. "Do you consider Dr. Fauci a danger to the American people?"

"I don't hear Dr. Fauci telling, saying that people should be taking hydroxychloroquine," Keilar said.

It's interesting to look back now and see how opinions about Fauci have changed since then. At the time of this CNN appearance of mine, he still had the image of the "good doctor" that Americans were looking to for guidance and reassurance. It wasn't until later that most Republicans soured on him, for his lies about mask wearing, his lies about funding gain-of-function research, and his defense of the Wuhan lab that likely caused the pandemic in the first place.

From here to the end of the conversation, there's so much crosstalk that I'll refer to the CNN transcript, which describes the action:

MURTAUGH: He [Fauci] had been asked a direct question—
(CROSSTALK)

MURTAUGH: —would you prescribe it? And he said yes. Go back and check your news archives.

KEILAR: I think we're pretty—

MURTAUGH: I think you'll find that to be the case.

KEILAR: I think—Tim, I think you're doing a real disservice to Americans.

I just want to be clear to everyone out there, we've talked to a number of doctors and experts, including federal experts. This is not something that you want to be playing with. All right: Studies have been canceled because this stuff is so dangerous.

Tim Murtaugh, thank you for coming on. It's good to see you again.

MURTAUGH: It has been used for 65 years. How dangerous could it possibly be? It is a known—it is a known—

(CROSSTALK)

KEILAR: It is an anti-malarial drug.

MURTAUGH: —that's been used for six and a half decades.

(CROSSTALK)

MURTAUGH: So how dangerous could it be?

(CROSSTALK)

MURTAUGH: You just said it is a dangerous drug but, yet, you admit it was used for 65 years. How dangerous could it be?

KEILAR: To prevent—to prevent malaria, not for people who potentially dying—

(CROSSTALK)

MURTAUGH: Well, is it dangerous or not? Will it kill you or not? You just said it was dangerous, yet, you admit that people take it for malaria. So is it dangerous or is it not?

KEILAR: I don't think people that are on their deathbed are given an anti-malarial medication to prevent them getting—you know what, Tim, no, we're done with this part—

(CROSSTALK)

MURTAUGH: So it's only used by people on their deathbed?

KEILAR: Tim—

MURTAUGH: Is that what you're saying?

KEILAR: We're done with this conversation. I think that you're just really confusing the situation. And it does no service to anyone's health especially.

Tim Murtaugh, with the Trump campaign.

MURTAUGH: There's a lot to be said for this interview, you're right.

Reading through this exchange again, years after it occurred, I am struck by how much the argument reveals how each of us viewed our role at the time. My place in the conversation was obvious: I was representing the president's re-election campaign, and therefore defended and promoted the work of his administration. Keilar's view of her role was obvious as well, but it wasn't what you might expect from a news anchor who supposedly wanted to inform viewers of facts, and not shape opinion.

It is impossible to read that transcript or watch a tape of the interview, and not conclude that Keilar, and therefore her bosses at CNN, viewed their role as the opposition. They were opposed to President Trump, opposed to his re-election, and opposed to the people who were working for him. Like most in the media, for them it did not matter the policy or issue being discussed; their starting position on every point was that Trump was wrong, and it was only a matter of figuring out how. That's not anything close to journalism.

Appearing on a show like that was an adrenaline rush, for sure, but it often left me feeling a bit disappointed. I liked the thrill of battle on live television, and I liked it when I knew I had landed some blows and scored some points, but it was upsetting to discover that there were some who held us in real disdain for the simple fact that we worked for Trump. Brianna Keilar, for example, made it plain that she found me personally objectionable because of the political candidate who employed me. That's also not professional journalism.

It was disappointing, because I'd known many reporters over the years in prior campaigns, most of whom held political views that were left of center. I had worked on a lot of races and had relationships with reporters in many states and at the national level, and I had mostly found that as professionals, we all knew the situation.

When I spoke for a campaign, I represented the views of that campaign or candidate, and not my own opinions. I was doing a job and playing a role, just as I would do for the next campaign that hired me. It is also true that I have always worked for candidates whose views aligned mostly with my own anyway. Most reporters were, likewise, doing the same thing. They would challenge me without being offensive or overtly partisan, and they played the role of an adversarial press, which is right and good and fine. Even when I had testy exchanges with reporters, I liked to think that we were still able to put it aside and have a working relationship.

But on the Trump campaign, I found that things were different. If they had not actively "put on the jersey" for the Democrats, the media were at least pulling in the same direction because they opposed President Trump so openly and forcefully. Brianna Keilar was just one example; there were many others.

Jim Sciutto, also of CNN, was another guy who was an obvious partisan, and every time I appeared on his show, he attacked aggressively from the very first word. He quite clearly viewed me as a political adversary and conducted interviews in what I felt was a condescending and accusatory manner.

One day in August 2020, I appeared on his show, and he repeatedly asked me if President Trump accepted responsibility for all the

American deaths attributable to COVID-19. This, obviously, was an unanswerable question in a political sense, which is exactly why he asked it.

If I said that the president did accept responsibility, then I would have agreed with the false narrative that Trump was responsible for the effects of a virus that came from China. Additionally, I'd have handed CNN the very soundbite it was looking for.

If I said he did not accept responsibility, it might sound callous and inconsistent, because we were simultaneously looking for credit for the president's overall response to the pandemic, and so we would be wanting the good without taking the bad. Any observer could see clearly that CNN's goal was not to be a mere journalistic outlet covering current events, but that it wanted to be an active participant in the political campaign.

In the end, I had to make a decision on the fly during a live interview, and so I blamed China and just repeatedly answered affirmatively about the president's record in fighting the coronavirus.

A month later, I went on with Sciutto again on the day of the first debate between President Trump and Joe Biden in Cleveland. Even though there was that big event later that night, Sciutto wanted to talk about President Trump's income taxes, some details of which had been reported by the *New York Times* two days earlier.

I had to fight through a series of almost indignant questions, and at one point gestured to the empty debate hall behind me at Cleveland's Case Western Reserve University and said, "Jim, are you aware that there's a debate tonight? Could we talk about that maybe?"

I recalled that someone had mentioned to me once that Sciutto had been a senior staffer for the US ambassador to China during the Obama administration. That meant that he had been a political appointee, which indicated that he was a partisan Democrat who had served in an administration to advance an agenda he embraced. That's a perfectly legitimate thing to do, but someone who had done it should not later pretend to be a non-partisan journalist like Sciutto was doing.

So, when we were talking about a tax refund that Trump had taken, I slipped it in.

"That refund that you're referring to was made possible under a law signed by your former boss, Barack Obama, that allows people to claim losses in previous years and carry them forward," I said.

Sciutto bristled immediately.

"Don't go personal here, Tim Murtaugh," he said. "Don't go personal here. I worked as chief of staff for the US ambassador to China."

"It's not personal, it's a fact," I said. "President Obama signed that law."

Point scored, but it's still ridiculous that anyone had to go into a television interview armed with little zingers like it was verbal professional wrestling.

I was booked to do an MSNBC hit with Katy Tur from Salt Lake City, the site of the vice presidential debate in early October 2020, and MSNBC demanded that I wear a mask during the live shot. Mind you, it was a bright and sunny day, and I was standing outside, easily more than six feet away from any crew the network could have been concerned about. Tur herself was in a studio somewhere else.

After it was confirmed that the mask was a condition of the live shot, I huddled over the phone with some of the campaign team back in Virginia to discuss whether I should proceed. As a group we decided that it was better to participate in the hit than to skip it, so I went through with it.

Tur wanted to focus on a tweet from President Trump, which included the lines, "Don't be afraid of Covid. Don't let it dominate your life." And it quickly became clear that Tur's tactic for this interview was to cite the names of people who had recently died from COVID-19 and ask me if they had been guilty of letting COVID-19 win.

And that's exactly how the interview went. Her initial question was keyed off a video she played from actress Amanda Kloots, whose husband, Nick Cordero, had died of the virus. Kloots was harshly critical of Trump's tweet, and I responded in the only way I could.

"The president and the campaign and everyone here, we all grieve of course for the families who have lost loved ones as a result of the virus," I said. "The president's point is that he wants people to take it seriously, he wants people to take precautions, but we cannot let it run our lives for us."

Tur was not to be put off her plan, however, and she proceeded to read what amounted to brief obituaries, asking me to respond to each one.

Here's an example of a lead-up to a question:

> The *New York Times* profiled a woman named Marny Xiong, a 31-year-old school board chair from Minnesota. They say when her father had trouble breathing in early May, but was afraid to go to the hospital, Miss Xiong offered to accompany him. But then the virus leveled her. On May 7th, they went to separate hospitals, both going on ventilators and intensive care. Her father, Zahoua Xiong, returned home on Memorial Day. Miss Xiong never came off the ventilator, never spoke to her family again. She died on June 7th.

And then Tur swung the hammer.

"Tim, what's the campaign's message to that Minnesota family?" she asked. "Marny Xiong died alone in the hospital. Did she let the virus dominate her?"

That wasn't journalism. It was the ghoulish exploitation of the deaths of real people so that Katy Tur could thrill the MSNBC audience by attacking someone from the Trump campaign. It was juvenile and a bad-faith effort to specifically blame one person—President Trump—for deaths caused by a global pandemic that began in China.

SWING HARD IN CASE YOU HIT IT

But the only TV hit I did in 2020 that people still mention to me today happened in late October on Chris Cuomo's show on CNN. It was a doozy, and not just because it was twelve minutes long, which is an eternity in TV hit terms.

Beforehand, as I did for a lot of the interviews that I expected to be difficult, I sat in Alexa Henning's office and did a bit of preparation. She put me through some harsh questioning to try to approximate what Cuomo would be like on the air.

After the brief prep session, I headed to the campaign's studio, which made me walk past Matt Wolking's office, from which he ran the communications War Room. He called me over and handed me a printed screenshot of Chris Cuomo interviewing his brother Andrew, the governor of New York at the time, during one of their many appearances together on CNN. The left side of the image showed Chris Cuomo holding up a giant cotton swab to make a joke about the size of his brother's nose. Andrew Cuomo was pictured grimacing on the right side of the picture.

Get it? It was a coronavirus testing gag, one Cuomo brother to another.

I got Wolking's intent immediately. I still smarted sometimes from my first appearance on Brianna Keilar's show, when she said there was no room for humor in the discussion of the coronavirus. Since that hit, I'd been kicking myself for not remembering how the Cuomo brothers regularly yucked it up on the air, which I could have used to undercut Keilar's apparent ban on anything of a humorous nature. Cuomo was sure to accuse Trump of failing to take the situation seriously enough, and the picture Wolking had given me was the perfect way to show that CNN had no problem making jokes of their own.

That's just the way the interview unfolded, with Cuomo repeatedly criticizing the Trump approach to the pandemic. At a certain point, I just picked my spot and held up the picture of Chris Cuomo and his gubernatorial brother.

"Does this look like a couple of guys who were taking it seriously?" I asked. "You had your brother on for the Cuomo Brothers Comedy Hour, joking about the size of the Q-Tip that you would need for his nose to take the test."

"Yeah, I did. It was funny as hell," Cuomo said.

I got in another good line a little later when I was hitting him for media reports that he was seen in public when he was supposed to be isolating while COVID-19 positive.

"We know you broke quarantine and went to the Hamptons," I said. "And then you came home and you pretended to rise up from your basement like Lazarus even though you had already broken quarantine while you were COVID positive."

Cuomo denied all of that, of course.

There was some Twitter buzz about that hit, and FoxNews.com and some other websites ran stories about the exchange, with Fox describing it as a "fiery spat." That was one that I was proud of, and a TV hit that I actually felt good about when it was over. Yes, I thought I had performed well, and I had used Wolking's prop to its intended effect, but it was more than that.

It was different from the Brianna Keilar, Jim Sciutto, or Katy Tur interviews, which really came off as bad-faith pissing matches and tedious attempts by the hosts to "own" the Trump campaign spokesman. I thought Cuomo was not the same because he actually acknowledged that we all had our own jobs and roles to play in our situations.

"I respect your effort because that's the game," Cuomo said as we wrapped up the long conversation. It may surprise some readers that I have to admit that I have a kind of grudging admiration for the guy.

Sometimes internal questions would come up about the utility of spending so much energy doing television appearances on shows and networks where the audience was extremely unlikely to even consider voting for President Trump. It was true that it was grueling to go through the preparation for such TV hits, and for me it was mostly just getting mentally ready for the fight rather than studying information, because it was like going into a verbal boxing match. The hits themselves were difficult and risky because it would be easy to say something embarrassing or damaging while under pressure. And the whole endeavor felt performative, especially when the anchors behaved as belligerently as any Democratic National Committee mouthpiece would.

But even if the audiences of these shows were hugely slanted against us, if we had a Trump campaign voice on there, it would likely be the only time all day that CNN or MSNBC viewers would hear our point of view. If fifteen seconds of our message managed to cut through the political bickering, maybe that counted as a success.

My many appearances on television were something of a concern for Dena because she had always been aware of the loss of privacy that comes with such a job. I figured that since I had been in political communications for years and had been quoted on the record frequently, my anonymity had been surrendered long before. Her view was that a presidential campaign was different, and the fact that I would appear on national television raised the whole thing to another level. This was yet something else that she was right about.

As proof that her worries had been valid, I started to receive hate mail every so often, delivered to our house in Alexandria, Virginia, usually after I had done a CNN hit. In fact, the messages often cited one of those appearances as the motivation for writing to me. While the notes never contained any explicit threats, they were angry enough to be worrisome, and the fact that the letter writers had gone to the trouble of finding my home address was disconcerting.

"Your CNN performance ignored the obvious. There is never a time when the President of the United States should be hyping any medicine for any purpose," read one letter, unsigned and postmarked from Eureka, California, on July 28, 2020. "I almost feel sorry for you that you have chosen to work for an incompetent, delusional sociopath—almost."

"Of course Donald Trump would tell us that the Earth is flat, and you would be on CNN with drawings of the flat earth," the writer concluded. "You need to get to confession, since your sins are mounting."

That last part could be construed as threatening, so I turned the letter in so the Secret Service could take a look. They said they would assess it, but if anything ever came of it, I never heard about it.

Another hate letter arrived at the campaign office, which was less intimidating than getting one at home, and it was signed by a person from Toronto—so, not even someone who could vote in our election. Regardless, the man had strong feelings.

Here's the letter in its entirety, because it really is a thing of beauty (bold in original):

Mr. Murtaugh:

I watched a part of your appearance on CNN last night. The grim expression on your face suggested you might be constipated which lines up with what you were saying. You're full of shit, but why would I expect otherwise from a **Donald Trump** supporter.

A global perspective says Mr. Trump is a dangerous idiot, a domestic terrorist, an international thug, a Russian stooge, and a failed businessman who wouldn't know truth if it fucked him up the ass dry. And, oh yes, he is personally responsible for the deaths of tens of thousands of Americans. That's only a start.

Odd though that there are people in the United States like you, large numbers of people who appear to be saying enthusiastically that, "Hey, this is the kind of person we want in the White House!

Where in hell is your moral compass?

Yours truly,
[redacted]

From his list of grievances about President Trump, I could clearly see that he was probably a frequent CNN watcher, because, profanity aside, these were the basic talking points that Brianna Keilar and many of her colleagues used daily. Of course, I didn't contact the guy, but I did wonder one thing, though: If he believed that President Trump was personally responsible for the deaths of Americans, then who was responsible for the deaths in Canada? Or in any other country?

On Twitter, there were plenty of insults to my basic humanity or cracks about my hairline. And my single favorite insult of all was from a guy who asked, "Tim, why do you look like a generic supervillain?"

Some people didn't like to read their hate tweets, but I mostly thought they were amusing. But there was one that bothered me, because it came from someone who should know better.

Paid CNN contributor Joe Lockhart had been White House press secretary to President Bill Clinton, and so he should understand the roles that professional political communicators play and the way we go about our jobs. I have had many political disagreements with staffers from other campaigns, and I never let any adversarial relationship slip outside the confines of the professional world. But Lockhart proved himself to be a hothead and someone who put politics above anything else.

On Twitter, Lockhart took aim at me and Trump White House press secretary Kayleigh McEnany, and offered his negative assessment of how we were performing in our jobs. All capitalization and punctuation here is from the original tweet of September 29, 2020:

I worked as Press Secretary to a President. If i ever acted like @PressSec i'd hope someone fired me. I also served as the Press Secretary to a President running for reelection. If i ever acted like

@TimMurtaugh I'd hope someone would take me outside and shoot me.

Fox News thought enough of this that it ran a story on its website with the headline, "CNN's Joe Lockhart suggests Kayleigh McEnany be fired, Tim Murtaugh be shot."

And they say that Republicans are responsible for the erosion of civility.

17

Rehab Again
2010

After I got canned by the RGA, I quickly decided to go to rehab again. I chose a beautiful place called Father Martin's Ashley (since renamed Ashley Addiction Treatment) near Havre de Grace, Maryland. Father Martin's, recommended to me by my aunt Kathy, was situated on almost 150 acres along the banks of the Chesapeake Bay in an idyllic setting. It's considered one of the top treatment centers in the country, and having spent a lot of time there, I certainly know why.

The twenty-eight-day program was well worth the time and effort, I believed, because it was a reordering of my priorities, the way I thought about alcohol and addiction, and the way I understood it as an actual disease and not a moral failing. A lot of the instruction we received was medical and biological in nature, and the spiritual and recovery-oriented counseling provided what I thought was a comprehensive treatment program.

Of course, I was a little apprehensive at the beginning, but as it was not my first time in residential rehab, I got into the swing of things quickly. After a few days in the detox ward, where new arrivals were closely monitored by a medical team for the dangerous effects of alcohol withdrawal, I was moved to a room with one other patient.

You meet all kinds of people in rehab, and my first roommate, a middle-aged guy from Texas, was the type who believed that he could control his drinking if someone would just teach him how. He told me on our first night as roomies that he hoped to be able to "learn to just drink red wine at dinner." I told him that I was no expert, but that I thought our counselors would try to dissuade him of the idea that any alcoholic can tolerate drinking "just a little bit." After less than a week, he checked himself out "against medical advice" like I had done back at Seabrook in New Jersey.

Until we were given the medical all-clear, new patients had to visit the nurses station multiple times a day so the nurses could check our vital signs and such. On the wall behind the station was a large dry-erase board that depicted the layout of the residential parts of the facility with the different buildings and rooms marked and numbered, and with patient names posted where their assigned beds were located. Most of the rooms showed two names in them, but there were a small number—maybe half a dozen—that appeared to be singles.

I asked around and discovered that it was the nurses themselves who made the room assignments, which told me that I needed to begin to strategically court them and make them my friends. From that point forward, I was upbeat and friendly, in contrast to some patients who were quiet, or even somewhat surly. Many of us were at Father Martin's voluntarily, but there were some who were there under court order or because they were compelled to surrender by their families.

After a few days getting to know the nurses better, I started to ask how room changes worked, and they said that it was like fitting a jigsaw puzzle together. There were slightly fewer than 120 patient beds, which meant that there were those who reached the end of their twenty-eight days fairly frequently. Sometimes people left early, or in rare cases were asked to leave for misbehavior of some kind. There were always new addicts showing up at the front door the same as I had, and there were some people who required special accommodation, like those who snored terribly.

"Do you snore?" a nurse asked me.

"Does that mean I have a better chance at a single room?" I asked in return.

"It certainly helps," she said.

"Then, yes," I replied. "I snore a lot."

In a matter of a week, I had my own room and felt like a king. It occurs to me now that this kind of scheming to wrangle a favorable room assignment might qualify as an example of alcoholic thinking, meaning that I was still focused on my personal wants instead of on my recovery. But it made for a much more comfortable stay, so I can't say that I regret it.

The food was excellent at Father Martin's, and you could eat as much as you wanted. They even held steak night every so often, and at mealtime it was frequently difficult to choose among the several featured entrées they offered. Caffeine was in limited supply, with our only access to it being a low-test brew of coffee that was only available for a few hours in the morning.

One time I asked a younger patient, who said he had been to seven other rehab facilities, how he thought Father Martin's compared to others he had seen.

"This is like 'Rehab by Sandals,'" he said approvingly, referring to the Caribbean resort company.

I felt there was a definite emotional arc to my twenty-eight days at Father Martin's Ashley. For the first half, I looked at my release date as being an eternity away. It seemed that the weeks stretched out before me like a treadmill without end. But by the time I passed the midpoint,

I began to look at the advancing days on the calendar as the whittling down of my time in this perfectly safe place. At the beginning, I couldn't wait to leave; by the end, I didn't want to go.

When I was ensconced at Father Martin's, my only responsibilities were to participate in my own recovery and not drink. That was it. There were no concerns about work, or bills, or where I had parked my car the night before. Those were real-world things that didn't intrude in there. We weren't even allowed to have cell phones and we only had access to email and the internet for an hour a week. We could read certain newspapers, like the *Baltimore Sun* or *Washington Post*, on Sundays. There were no televisions anywhere.

But we didn't need those distractions because they kept us pretty busy. There was a community meeting every morning that provided a message of sobriety before breakfast was served. And then we had workshops, meetings, and group therapy sessions. There was always a lecture on the medical and physiological aspects of addiction, and we learned what the substances we abused did to our brains. There was a three-hour break in the early afternoon where you could engage in exercise or take a yoga class, or just take a nap. I usually opted for the latter.

In the evenings after dinner, we either held our own AA meetings in the lecture hall, or we rode as a group on a shuttle bus to go to a meeting in the town of Havre de Grace. After that, there'd be decaffeinated coffee and snacks for a brief period in the cafeteria. Sometimes people played board games or listened to someone playing the guitar. Lights out was at 11 p.m. The schedule on the weekends was a little lighter, but there were classes and meetings just the same.

I began keeping a journal for the first time, which we were encouraged to do, and I wrote more personal letters to friends and family in those four weeks than I had ever otherwise produced across all the years of my life. I was on the beam, I was getting stronger and healthier, and I felt good. I took to waking up early to watch the sun rise over the Chesapeake Bay.

Dena visited twice, on what they called Family Day, which was a little awkward because we truly had not been dating for that long. There were workshops and lectures that families were asked to attend, and I think they made Dena uncomfortable. She had done more than anyone else in supporting me and taking care of me through all my troubles, but I think she was uneasy with the idea of taking counseling as well.

I recognized that I was asking a tremendous amount from her, and that she was giving more than I rightly had reason to expect. I felt guilty then, and still do now, that my lifelong history of making bad decisions had caused her to be in the undesirable position of helping to clean up after the chronic selfish behavior of another. As good boyfriends go, I was not one. But without her I would have been completely lost.

My mom and dad also visited, as did my brother, and I tried to keep those conversations lively by giving them an enthusiastic tour of the place like I was a proud freshman showing off my college campus. I remember feeling reluctant to describe what deep thoughts I had been thinking about my addiction, or anything describing my counseling beneath the superficial. It was easier to show the optimism and sense of recovery that I truly did feel emerging.

Even so, as I walked out after completing the program, I feared it wouldn't be long at all before I started drinking again.

18

Identifying with Parscale
September 2020

As my plane touched down in Cleveland on a Sunday night, two days before the first presidential debate of 2020, a text appeared on my phone from Trump campaign senior strategist Jason Miller.

"Call me," it said. He didn't need to add "ASAP," like a lot of people would do. The two-word directive was sufficient to convey urgency.

Once we made it to the gate, I pulled my luggage from the overhead bin and waited for the attendants to open the plane's door. While I stood, I dialed Miller.

"Where are you?" he said by way of greeting.

"I just landed in Cleveland," I said. "Still on the plane and can't really speak freely. What's up?"

"Something is happening with Brad at his house," Miller said in quick, clipped words. "There's a hostage situation or something. There are cops outside his house. We don't know exactly what's going on."

"Holy shit," I said. "What are we supposed to do?"

"Call me when you can talk," he said, and hung up.

After I had made my way to the rideshare area at Cleveland Hopkins International, I called Jason back.

"Okay, I know a little more now," he said, and explained the terrible story.

Brad's wife, Candice, whom we all knew, had called the Fort Lauderdale police because Brad had been acting erratically. She told the authorities that Brad had a gun, and that she feared that he was suicidal. There had been a brief standoff of some kind, not really a hostage situation, and Brad had been taken into custody unarmed. He had been intoxicated and arrested under some provisions in the law governing mental illness.

"Oof," I said. "Is he okay, do you know?"

"I don't," Miller replied.

"Are we being asked to comment?"

"Not yet, but Florida media is on the case and so it's going to get out. We need to issue a statement. Should come from you."

"Okay," I said. "Gimme a couple minutes and I'll text you something."

Between me and Miller, we worked out a simple statement and let it fly.

It read, simply, "Brad Parscale is a member of our family and we all love him. We are ready to support him and his family in any way possible."

That statement made it to a lot of media outlets, and I think I was just sending the quote to each reporter who asked, rather than sending it out in a press release email blast. But before I had made it from the airport to the hotel in an Uber, Miller called back.

"What's up?" I asked.

Miller said, "The president had a revision for your quote and he wants you to make sure that everyone gets this new version."

"Okay," I said, because that was the word from the boss. "Send me the new quote and I'll get it around."

When I received it, I wasn't surprised at the pivot President Trump wanted to make. He had added some language that swiped at our political opponents and blamed them for hounding Parscale into his personal situation.

Here was the entire revised quote:

"Brad Parscale is a member of our family and we all love him. We are ready to support him and his family in any way possible. The disgusting, personal attacks from Democrats and disgruntled RINOs have gone too far, and they should be ashamed of themselves for what they've done to this man and his family."

Some reporters noted that we had issued two different quotes, one more combative than the other, and CNN's Chris Cillizza wrote a column describing the second version as "disgusting." But after that first night, my two statements faded from memory.

It wasn't long before the local police released body camera footage from the officers on the scene at Brad's house. It showed Brad ambling over to officers at the foot of his driveway, holding a beer while shirtless and wearing only shorts. He calmly attempted to describe his version of events before officers off-camera shouted at him to get on the ground. When he failed to obey immediately, an officer rushed him from the side and tackled him. Other officers swarmed, and Parscale was taken into custody.

Before I sat down to write about this time period for this book, I had not seen that video since it was first released, and it was as painful for me to watch as the first time. I know that Brad is a large guy, but it seemed to me that there had not been any need to take him down so violently.

It was so difficult to see because I felt like I knew a little about what Brad might have been going through. I can't know exactly what his situation was, what his thoughts were, or whether drinking was a significant problem for him or not. But I knew that I had hit rock bottom once, and I figured that Brad had also just experienced the worst day of his own life.

Brad's story was a little different, of course, because most of us are not unlucky enough for video of our worst moment to be played in an endless loop by national cable news hosts who hate us. I waited until I knew that he had been released from custody and called him. It wasn't a long conversation, but I conveyed that I thought that I knew how he felt, and I let him vent a little bit. Today, I am glad to know that those troubles are apparently behind him.

Brad was the one who brought me onto the Trump 2020 campaign in the first place, giving me the responsibility of leading communications for the re-election of the president of the United States, and I'll always be grateful for that. I would never have experienced any of this without him, and that would have been terrible.

19

Living with An Alcoholic
2010 and 2011

After I got out of Father Martin's, Dena asked me to move in with her—I believe because she didn't think I should just be discarded as a person and also so she could try to keep an eye on me. It was an amazing display of love and compassion, and it gave me hope that I could really get things together. We lived in her condominium south of Old Town Alexandria, and we even got a rescue dog, a male brindle beagle mix puppy we named Ollie, who Dena hoped would help me in my recovery.

There's a saying among alcoholics that while we're inside a safe place like a treatment facility, our addiction is outside in the parking lot doing pushups to get stronger for the next battle. If that's true for most people, then my addiction had been training for the Olympic weightlifting team while I was at Father Martin's, because it came back at me more forcefully than ever before.

There were really only two things that I was supposed to be doing: going to Alcoholics Anonymous meetings and looking for a job. I did both of those things sometimes, but I also spent a lot of time sneaking off to the ABC store to buy Jägermeister. I had to find a lot of creative places to hide my bottles, but as any alcoholic knows, we are very clever and resourceful people.

There was a laundry room in the basement level of Dena's condo building, where I had noticed that the dryers had hollow spaces along their bottoms that were accessible from the back. They were the perfect hidey holes for bottles of Jäger, and it became my routine to excuse myself from the apartment to take Ollie for a walk and stop by the laundry room coming and going.

There were large boxwoods and other big bushes all over the condominium property, some with ivy around their beds, which all made fine hiding spots for bottles. It was important to identify a landmark of some kind to pinpoint the location of the hidden booze, or valuable time could be spent feeling around in the greenery for the bottle. It was embarrassing to think that I could be seen by the neighbors while doing that as well.

I developed a method of hiding bottles inside the one-bedroom apartment, which was tricky business in such a small place, by using the clothes already hanging in the closet. A bottle tucked into the inside pocket of a suit jacket is completely undetectable unless you start feeling around. I used that strategy a lot, and at random intervals I changed which jacket I was using for the hiding spot.

One day I walked into the small dining room of the place, and Dena was standing there with her arms folded, staring at a bottle of Jägermeister she had placed on the table.

"What's that?" I asked, genuinely surprised.

"You tell me," she said. "What is it doing in this apartment?"

"I don't know where you found it," I said. "I guarantee you I didn't know that bottle was here. If I had known it was here, it would be empty. That bottle isn't empty."

It amazes me today that I ever thought that was a good defense. Dena threw the bottle away in disgust.

I was piecing together contract work as a "consultant" again, doing some things for a conservative grassroots group called Americans for Prosperity, as well as for a few candidates for the General Assembly. It didn't keep me very busy, but it brought in a couple thousand dollars every month, which was about the amount of drinking money I needed. I wasn't paying Dena any rent and I rarely bought groceries. If we went out, I would only occasionally be able to buy dinner or movie tickets.

I was a real treat to have around.

In June 2011, I went out drinking one night and somehow ended up a few developments over from our place, banging on the door of a retirement community center at 1 a.m. Today I still have no idea how I found my way there, or why, because I've never had a connection to the place. I suppose I was just disoriented and lost.

When the police arrived, finding me intoxicated and alarmingly disheveled, they arrested me and took me to the station until I sobered up. They towed my car, but couldn't charge me with drunk driving because they hadn't seen me operating the vehicle. Since I was not capable of making a coherent statement, they just charged me with public drunkenness and assessed a fine and some fees.

During this disgraceful period, it felt like I was having a run-in with law enforcement every few months. There would be a public drunkenness citation, or at least an admonition that I had to move along and get myself home safely. I was spiraling out of control and my descent was only picking up speed.

20

The Cleveland Debate
September 2020

The Commission on Presidential Debates (CPD) was not favorable to the Trump campaign. We thought that everyone knew that, but no one would say it out loud except us.

At Bill Stepien's instruction, I started writing what would turn into a series of letters to the CPD, beginning in August 2020. We were making what I thought were serious and legitimate arguments about the timing of the events themselves.

Because so many states had adopted early voting that began many weeks before election day, the first debate, scheduled for September 29 in Cleveland, would occur after as many as eight million Americans in sixteen states had already started voting. By the time of the third and final debate, set for October 22 in Nashville, as many as forty-nine million Americans in thirty-four states would have been voting for weeks.

We sent a letter to the CPD, signed by former New York City mayor Rudy Giuliani, our liaison dealing with the members of the

Commission. We suggested adding an additional debate earlier in the schedule so that at least one such event would take place before anyone started voting anywhere. And we offered a list of potential moderators, of which many, but not all, were culled from conservative news outlets.

"Simply put, the Commission's current approach is an outdated dinosaur and not reflective of voting realities in 2020," our letter read. "For a nation already deprived of a traditional campaign schedule because of the COVID-19 global pandemic, it makes no sense to also deprive so many Americans of the opportunity to see and hear the two competing visions for our country's future before millions of votes have been cast."

To my surprise, the Commission responded within a day, and expressed openness to an additional event, "if the candidates were to agree that they wished to add to that schedule." While we knew that Biden would never agree to a fourth debate, we replied immediately and took a few shots at our opponent. We were also making these letters available to the media as we went along.

"While we do understand that Mr. Biden has been sequestered in his basement in Wilmington, Delaware for some time, President Trump still believes that the American people deserve to see the candidates for president side by side at some point," our letter read, again signed by Giuliani.

It's an accepted rule of thumb that the candidate who calls for more debates is the one who is losing, and that wasn't necessarily untrue in this case. Yes, we wanted more debates, and we wanted them earlier, because we believed that most Americans were not aware of how much Biden had deteriorated mentally and physically since they had seen him as vice president. Because he had the luxury of staying off the campaign trail due to COVID-19, he'd been able to stay mostly under wraps—but in a debate, there would be no place to hide.

Two weeks later, we sent a follow-up letter from Giuliani, reiterating our desire to add a debate earlier in the schedule. We made the same arguments as before, and then I added in a little joke at the bottom where we carbon copied Biden.

After Giuliani's signature, the letter included:

CC: Fmr. Vice President Joe Biden
Basement
Wilmington, DE

I was so proud of that.

Our correspondence changed nothing, of course, but it built a record that we could cite when we inevitably had to complain about the formats, rules, topics, and moderators.

As the date of the first debate neared, there was a flurry of last-minute meetings to negotiate the finer details of the matchup between President Trump and Joe Biden, which was to take place in Cleveland. Our negotiator was a guy named Max Miller, who gave off an air of being fearless and had come over to the campaign from the White House, where he'd been an aide to the president, filling many roles.

A few days before the event, we had a campaign debate preparation meeting and Max gave us a rundown of how his last negotiating session had gone. He went through a list of different things that he had demanded, and that the Biden campaign had requested, and the things to which both sides had agreed. At the end, he had just one more item.

"So, as we were wrapping up, I said to them, 'Oh, also, we'll be wanting to do an earpiece check,'" Max said. There was silence in the room for a moment.

"What?" someone said.

"An earpiece check," Max repeated. "I told them that we wanted both candidates to submit to an examination right before they take the stage to make sure they aren't wearing earpieces."

"Jesus Christ, Max!" someone laughed.

As I recall, I was assured that the Biden camp had agreed to the ear check, so on the morning of the debate, we accused Biden's team of backing out of the deal.

"Joe Biden's handlers several days ago agreed to a pre-debate inspection for electronic earpieces but today abruptly reversed themselves and declined," I told Bloomberg News.

The Biden team merely dismissed the demand as a "distraction," however the second sentence of the Bloomberg piece was exactly what we wanted.

"The assertion by the president's team that a third-party inspection of the candidates' ears is necessary is part of the Trump campaign's contention that Biden is not mentally fit for the debate," it read.

Score one for Max Miller, who would go on to capture the Republican nomination for Ohio's Seventh Congressional District, win the general election in 2022, and be sworn in as a member of the US House of Representatives on January 3, 2023.

By the time the big event in Cleveland finally rolled around, the RealClearPolitics average of national polls gave Biden a lead of about seven points nationally, so we were looking for a strong performance from the president.

When it started, President Trump came out aggressively, and from the backstage war room I was hopeful. But the president attacked and interrupted repeatedly, and Biden attacked and hurled insults, and both candidates ended up duking it out for the duration of the night.

Perhaps the biggest news kernel that came out of the debate, aside from the overall food fight tone, was the exchange the president had with moderator Chris Wallace, then of Fox News. Wallace challenged Trump to specifically condemn white supremacy groups and prompted him with the name Proud Boys.

"Proud Boys, stand back and stand by," Trump said before pivoting. "But I'll tell you what, somebody's got to do something about Antifa and the left."

It was the consensus in our war room that Wallace had participated in the debate as a third combatant, not as a moderator, and our comments to the press afterward made heavy reference to that complaint. We explained that the president's message to groups like the Proud Boys was that they should stop what they were doing. And we pointed out how Trump had repeatedly condemned racist groups in the past already.

To FoxNews.com, I said that Trump had condemned white supremacy "over and over and over again."

"Just last week, the president declared the KKK a terrorist organization and it cannot be any more clear than that," I said.

I don't think many Americans knew who the Proud Boys were, but the exchange about them in that debate was what the media harped on, even though it had been a moment created by the moderator.

On television shows, we started telling hosts that Trump had beaten two opponents in the debate that night: Joe Biden and Chris Wallace.

21

 ## Three Jobs in One Year
2012

I remember looking so hard to find work that was meaningful to me that I called Branch Rickey III again, as I had learned that he had become the president of the Pacific Coast League in baseball's Triple-A minor league level. He advised that I could start at the ground level in baseball, but that I was pretty far along in my career for a change at that point. I don't know if his enthusiasm for my call was tempered by the fact that it was obvious that I was talking to him from inside a crowded bar.

Amazingly, I received a lifeline from my old boss George Allen, who was by then a former senator who had lost his re-election bid in 2006. In 2012, Allen would be running for his old seat again, facing Tim Kaine, now a former governor himself, in the November election. Early in the year, the Allen campaign brought me on in an undefined communications capacity, and I joined a small team working out of Allen's own private office in Old Town Alexandria.

Needless to say, my personal choices had not improved with the acceptance of a new job, and I fell into the familiar routine of drinking, working, and then drinking some more. I tried to avoid day drinking, because we worked in close quarters in the office, and I was sure someone would smell me.

One Saturday night, I found myself in Fredericksburg, although I don't remember why I had gone there in the first place. I got a hotel room near the highway, making sure that it was walking distance from a Chili's restaurant with a bar, and parked my car for the night. The next thing I knew, I was waking up in a holding cell, unsure of where I was or what had happened.

I had caught another public intoxication charge at the bar near the hotel and had been taken into custody so that I could sleep it off in the lockup. After they verified that I was sober again, hours later, they let me pay my fine, told me how to get my car out of the impound lot, and let me go.

I checked the internet for the Fredericksburg newspaper and found that it published lists of local arrests several times a week, so first thing Monday morning I called down and got a news editor on the phone. Without disclosing my name, I explained that if my name appeared in the newspaper as having been arrested, I would likely lose my job as well as my entire career. The editor expressed empathy, and sounded sincere, but ultimately explained that he couldn't change newspaper policy. The names would go in the paper if they appeared in the police reports, and that was going to be the final answer.

A day later, I found my entry on the Fredericksburg website and carried a sick feeling around with me all day. At work, I pretended nothing was wrong, and went about my business as normal. I told myself that if I got through the day unscathed, my chances of escaping serious repercussions dramatically improved. Throughout the hours of the workday, nothing happened, and I got home halfway believing I would survive.

After dinner, my cell phone rang and I saw the name Betsy Beamer, a longtime Allen aide who had served in his cabinet when he was governor. She was a senior advisor on the campaign, so it was not completely abnormal that she would call me. The timing, however, was a little too coincidental to be happenstance.

"Hey, there," I said, trying to sound alert and cheerful.

"I'm just gonna come right out and ask you," Beamer said, starting in right away. "Are you the same Tim Murtaugh who was arrested in Fredericksburg Saturday night?"

For one brief moment, I considered making up a lie, but just as quickly abandoned the idea.

"Yes," I said simply. "I thought about coming to you about it but I—I just didn't know what to do."

She sighed, and said, "I'm so sorry about this. But you know we're going to have to let you go from the campaign, right?"

Of course, they had to fire me. The only remotely positive thing was that my presence on the campaign had never been announced, and I had yet to be quoted on the record in any news stories about the race. When I was separated from the campaign, it was almost like I had never even been there.

The good news was that it was still early in a federal election year, and there were plenty of congressional races that were just staffing up. I managed to latch onto one near West Point, New York—the re-election campaign of Representative Nan Hayworth, an ophthalmologist turned conservative politician—and moved up there right away.

It was a short-lived stay. I had found a couple of bars I liked along the street near the apartment the campaign had rented me, but I never got comfortable with the job. There were some local consultants whose roles I didn't fully understand, and I felt right away that I would always be marginalized as an outsider. I decided to flee before too much time had passed.

I called Chris LaCivita, lied to him that I'd been sober for two months, and asked him if he knew of any candidates who needed campaign comms help. He said that he did, as a matter of fact, and how soon could I be in Connecticut?

Before the week was out, I was the new communications director for Linda McMahon, who, along with her husband Vince, had founded WWE, or World Wrestling Entertainment. She was running for Senate in Connecticut for the second time, having run unsuccessfully two years earlier.

Because I assumed that it was possible that everyone knew about my recent employment troubles associated with alcohol, I determined to keep a low profile while working in the New Haven area. I never went to bars, never ordered alcohol when out for dinner, and when I stopped to pick up bottles of Jägermeister for home consumption, I made sure to change liquor stores with regularity. I did keep a bottle hidden in my office, but that was a necessity.

Things were actually going well, because I felt like I had achieved a good balance between work and booze. I needed to maintain a certain blood alcohol level throughout the day, otherwise I started to feel sick. But I could function, didn't seem outwardly intoxicated, and I had a pretty good handle on what my drinking pace needed to be. I felt like I finally had alcoholism mastered.

Then one weekend, I decided to go to a casino. Because I was making good money, I got a nice room for two nights and took out plenty of cash for poker. I made it to the tables for a good long run Friday night, drinking free casino drinks the whole way through.

Saturday morning was painful, but I'd brought some Jäger with me and I was able to feel better after a pick-me-up shot, or two. Before too long, I was cruising again and looking forward to a responsibility-free weekend. I took drink after drink as I slowly got ready to leave the room and go back down for more poker.

Somehow, just as I stood at the edge of drunken oblivion again, I remembered that there was one small task I still had to take care of that morning. I had scheduled Linda McMahon to be on a local radio show, and she liked me to call her on her cell phone and connect her to the host using the conference feature on my iPhone.

The morning shots had gotten me hammered, and I know I was slurring my words as I got the candidate on the phone. I had trouble remaining focused, and I know I botched any attempt at communicating in normal conversational terms. It would have been obvious to McMahon and to the radio station that I was severely drunk.

After the radio hit, I abandoned the idea of going to play poker and climbed back into bed for a much-needed nap. I heard my phone vibrating with an incoming call, but I ignored it and passed out for a good long time.

Hours later, I woke up and looked with dread at my phone. There were several missed calls from the campaign manager, Corry Bliss, and a voice mail from Chris LaCivita. I played the message from LaCivita first.

"I can't help you if you don't call me back," he said on the recording, and hung up.

There was no avoiding it, so I clicked to return the call from Bliss.

"Linda said you sounded drunk this morning," he said as soon as he answered. He wasn't the kind of guy who spent much time tiptoeing around topics.

I remained silent.

He said, "Do you have an excuse?"

I paused. "No," I said, finally.

He waited a moment, and then said, "You're fired." And he hung up.

Because my flame-out on the McMahon campaign happened to roughly coincide with her winning the Republican primary against a former congressman, my departure could be explained by the shift into the general election season. It was conceivable that I had been hired only to assist her during the primary election period.

McMahon would go on to lose in the 2012 general election, as she had in 2010, and years later serve in the Trump Cabinet as the head of the Small Business Administration. I developed a lot of respect for her during that campaign and in the many times I interacted with her in Trump World. And I regret that she was yet another employer to whom I'd not shown the proper level of respect through my behavior.

I went back to Alexandria in my familiar status as an unemployed guy trying to beat an addiction that got the best of him most days. Without a job to keep me occupied, I returned to AA meetings in the hope that I could recapture some of the feelings of confidence and recovery I remembered from Father Martin's.

At the Serenity Club in Alexandria, a storefront that hosted AA meetings throughout the course of every day, I found a bunch of people from extremely varied backgrounds all working toward the same thing: lasting sobriety. They each just wanted to get through each day without picking up a drink. Almost to a person, they talked about taking life as it came, in very small increments, over and over again, one day at a time.

It was mostly just a large empty space with a bunch of mismatched chairs and tables, with a coffee machine against one wall and a lectern in one corner. I went to a meeting, which turned into many meetings, and I eventually found my first real AA sponsor, a wise old fellow named Peter. He said that he had mostly been a pot smoker but knew he needed to quit alcohol too, and that he had been sober for more than ten thousand days, which was more than twenty-seven years, if you did the math.

In an effort to show Dena that I was serious about finally trying to quit drinking, I increased my meeting attendance and started to meet regularly with Peter, one on one, to begin to go through the "Twelve Steps" of Alcoholics Anonymous. Except that I could never keep it together for very long, and I would constantly have to crawl back to Dena, and then Peter, after each time I slipped and got drunk again.

I can't explain why Dena continued to stand by me, despite all the evidence screaming to her that she should cut me loose. From what I knew about her, she didn't have any sort of savior complex in any other aspect of her life. I guess maybe she just saw something in me she thought was redeemable and did not believe in just throwing people away. Whatever the reason, I certainly didn't deserve her devotion to me, and I can never show her enough gratitude.

22

 POTUS Gets COVID-19, One Debate Gets Canceled While the Last One Proceeds
October 2020

I was just about to enter the studio in the campaign office for an evening television hit on Thursday, October 1, 2020, when word arrived that President Trump and First Lady Melania Trump had tested positive for COVID-19. The information was not yet public, and I was advised that the president would be the one to announce the news to the world, probably via Twitter, which could come at any moment.

This was a development that we long thought was possible, even probable, since most people felt that everyone would be infected sooner or later. There were going to be significant concerns about the health of the Trumps, particularly for the president, because, well, he was the president, and he was at a relatively advanced age, which put him in a demographic which statistically was more susceptible to the disease.

As I sometimes did when an unexpected piece of news (or a particularly hot tweet from Trump) appeared right before I was to go on

167

television, I trudged over to Bill Stepien's office to run the scenario past him.

"You heard about the president testing positive?" I asked Bill.

"Yup," he said, looking up. "What's up?"

"I have to be on TV in a few minutes," I explained.

"Of course you do." Stepien sighed. "Is it public yet?"

"I don't think so, but it could break before I go on, or it could come out while I'm on the air," I said.

"Well, he's the one who's got to announce it, so don't get ahead of him," he said. "And if you have to address it, then he's going to beat it, simple as that. He'll beat COVID, right?"

"Got it," I said, and headed back to the studio for makeup with our in-house makeup artist, Jessie D'Angelo, whose work had been seen on Fox News, CNN, all the networks, and in many motion pictures and TV shows.

Through a small miracle, the news of Trump's COVID-19 diagnosis did not break before or during my hit, and I was able to escape without having to react to it live on national television. Trump himself would indeed tweet about it a little later, at 12:54 a.m.

"Tonight, @FLOTUS and I tested positive for COVID-19," the tweet read. "We will begin our quarantine and recovery process immediately. We will get through this TOGETHER!"

The excitement among the press corps, even in the dead of night, was palpable and you could feel their eagerness to report on an illness contracted by Trump, which many of them felt he deserved.

"If he becomes sick, it could raise questions about whether he should remain on the ballot at all," the *New York Times* wrote. "Even if he does not become seriously ill, the positive test could prove devastating to his political fortunes given his months of diminishing the seriousness of the pandemic even as the virus was still ravaging the country and killing about 1,000 more Americans every day."

The *Washington Post* got into the he-deserved-it act as well, chiding the president for failing to signal his virtue by wearing a mask, despite competing opinions about their effectiveness.

"Even as the virus exploded around the nation, Trump has continued to hold large events featuring mostly maskless crowds of people who squeezed together to greet the president," the *Post* reported. "Trump has regularly appeared in public and in private without a mask, and has mocked Biden for wearing one and for curbing his campaign events. Many of Trump's aides also have eschewed masks, both in the West Wing presidential offices and on trips."

On MSNBC, Associated Press reporter Jonathan Lemire strongly implied that he thought Trump was the victim of karma.

"It completely upends everything the president has said on the virus this entire time," Lemire said. "He has time and again denied the seriousness of the pandemic, suggested that the nation was rounding the corner and on its last legs with battling this virus, flying in the face of science and been wrong over and over. And now, of course, he has contracted it."

During the hit, Lemire also admonished Trump for publicly claiming that children were less vulnerable to the coronavirus, which we now know to be true.

The president was admitted to Walter Reed National Military Medical Center after his positive test, and naturally it was the biggest news story in the world. The media covered it extensively, as they should have, but they couldn't contain their outrage at times. There was an eruption of angry stories after Trump briefly left the hospital for a ride around the block to wave to supporters because Secret Service agents were in the vehicle with him.

It was later revealed that the outing had been discussed extensively with doctors beforehand, and that the agents with the president had been wearing the same protective gear as frontline medical workers. But the media outrage machine could not be stopped.

Three days later, Trump returned to the White House and removed his mask in full view of television cameras, prompting further media fury. The president was trying to encourage the country to face the pandemic rather than cower from it, and he made that plain in a video message to the American people relating his personal experience with the virus.

"Don't let it dominate you," Trump said. "Don't be afraid of it."

CNN posted a story—not labeled as an opinion piece, mind you— that wailed that Trump had "staged a reckless departure" from the hospital "before posing for a mask-less photo-op on the White House balcony."

The reporters who filed the piece—Kevin Liptak and Maeve Reston—either missed the president's point or willfully ignored it.

"It was a remarkable attempt to convert his still-ongoing disease into a show of strength," they wrote, apparently oblivious to the president's signal to the country that we should be able to move forward despite the pandemic. It may not have been palatable to the media because it was Donald Trump saying it, but it was true that Americans had to return to a semblance of normal life as quickly as possible.

It was because of Trump's COVID-19 status that the second debate, scheduled for October 15 in Miami, was ultimately canceled. The Commission on Presidential Debates had decided that it would host the debate virtually because of Trump's illness, but our team objected to letting Biden off the hook with a remote appearance and we suggested rescheduling it. When that idea was rejected, the event was simply scrapped.

But even a canceled debate was not without controversy, as a dustup arose when Steve Scully, the C-SPAN television host who had been slated to moderate the debate, posted a tweet that raised some eyebrows in Trump World.

After Trump had attacked Scully as a "Never Trumper," in part because he had briefly been a young intern for Biden in the Senate, Scully tweeted, "@Scaramucci should I respond to trump."

The message was aimed at former White House communications director Anthony Scaramucci, who had served in that job for eleven days and had subsequently emerged as a Trump critic who was frequently highlighted by the media. We took the Scully tweet as evidence that he was colluding with the president's enemies and was therefore obviously too hostile to serve as moderator. For a week, Scully claimed that his Twitter account had been hacked, but then relented and admitted to having sent the message himself.

"Out of frustration, I sent a brief tweet addressed to Anthony Scaramucci," Scully finally said in a statement. "The next morning when I saw that this tweet had created a new controversy, I falsely claimed that my Twitter account had been hacked."

Scully was subsequently suspended but would return to C-SPAN in January 2021 and eventually resume hosting his show. He would leave C-SPAN for good in July that year.

Just over a week before the final debate in Nashville, the *New York Post* splashed a huge story across its front page revealing the existence of a laptop belonging to Joe Biden's son, Hunter. The computer was remarkable because of the data it contained, some of which linked Joe Biden to Hunter's lucrative business of selling access to his powerful father. Most of the money flowed to Hunter after meetings with super wealthy businessmen from China, Russia, Ukraine, Mexico, and Kazakhstan. The laptop and its contents would become an ongoing theme for the closing weeks of the campaign, in one form or another.

I want to reiterate that I viewed it as completely legitimate to go after Hunter Biden because of his lucrative deals with billionaires around the world, and because of how his father was implicated in all those schemes. As mentioned previously, I never sought to attack Hunter for things directly related to his addiction, or for his condition of being an addict. I knew what it was like to be controlled by a substance, and I wanted to stay away from bashing him for that. But anything involving foreign payments that could have involved his father were totally in bounds.

We sent another letter to the CPD, this time signed by campaign manager Bill Stepien, noting that the final debate on October 22 was supposed to be about foreign policy, but the topics released went well outside that area.

> We understand that Joe Biden is desperate to avoid conversations about his own foreign policy record, especially since President Trump has secured historic peace agreements among Israel, the United Arab Emirates, and Bahrain. New information recently revealed indicates that Biden himself was mentioned as a financial beneficiary of a deal arranged by his son Hunter and a communist Chinese-related energy company. If a major party candidate for President of the United States is compromised by the Communist Party of China, this is something Americans deserve to hear about, but it is not surprising that Biden would want to avoid it.

We also objected to the possibility that the CPD would be giving an unnamed debate official a "mute button" with the authority to shut off a candidate's microphone if the official believed that rules were being violated.

Naturally, our concerns were ignored again, but we had blasted away at the Commission once more, in the ongoing effort to cement for the public the campaign's view that the debate organizers were hopelessly and unfairly aligned with our opponent.

Once debate day finally arrived, the campaign still had a curve-ball to throw in the form of a pre-show surprise guest. In a press conference engineered by Jason Miller, former Biden family business associate Tony Bobulinski tore apart Joe Biden's claim that he had no knowledge of his son Hunter's foreign business schemes.

It had long been the contention of the Trump campaign that Hunter Biden enriched himself and his entire family by selling prox-imity to his father, including during the years that Joe Biden served as vice president. Joe Biden had insisted that he had never spoken to his son about his business dealings, which involved Hunter accepting large amounts of money from foreign businessmen, often in industries in which he had no expertise.

Bobulinksi took issue with Joe Biden's claim of ignorance, saying in our press conference, "I have heard Joe Biden say that he has never discussed business with Hunter. That is false. I have firsthand knowl-edge of this because I directly dealt with the Biden family, including Joe Biden."

The Navy veteran also cited an email from Hunter's laptop which discussed a payout for "the big guy" in a financial arrangement with a Chinese energy company. Bobulinski said that was a direct reference to the elder Biden.

Amazingly, in reporting on the press conference, ABC News referred to the accusations as "unsubstantiated," despite Bobulinski's repeated statements that he had been an eyewitness to many of the conversations among Biden family members. Bobulinski *was* the sub-stantiation of the information contained in the emails and texts on the laptop.

In the debate itself, the most significant parts to me were Presi-dent Trump's attempts to place Hunter's laptop front and center for the homestretch. And the way Joe Biden responded gave us a glimpse at how that storyline was going to go as we raced for the finish line.

"Don't give me this stuff about how you're this innocent baby," Trump said about the implications of the information on the laptop. "They are calling you a corrupt politician."

Biden replied, citing a letter that had recently appeared in the press, "There are 50 former national intelligence folks who said that what he's accusing me of is [misinformation from] a Russian plant," Biden said of Trump. "Five former heads of the CIA, both parties, say what he's saying is a bunch of garbage."

Biden was overstating the argument, but he was referencing a letter that had just been published by *Politico*, signed by fifty-one former American intelligence officials who said that the laptop story as reported by the *New York Post* had all the hallmarks of a Russian disinformation campaign. There will be more on the media's dismissal of the laptop later in this book, but at that point in the closing stretch of the campaign, the way that debate exchange was often reported was foretelling.

CNN ran a "fact check" under the title "Did Trump spread Russian disinformation during the debate?"

New York magazine had a piece headlined, "Trump Tries to Make 'Laptop from Hell' the New Hillary Emails. It Won't Work."

The *New York Times* ran a fact check on the claim that Biden was "the big guy" referenced in the Chinese energy deal with Hunter and rated it "misleading" simply because the Biden campaign denied it.

NBC News also published an item on Trump's repeated references to the Biden family financial activities, dismissing them as fringe rantings.

"The president's claims appear to be rooted in far-right conspiracy theories that the business dealings of the former vice president's son, Hunter Biden, were somehow funneling foreign dollars to the vice president and the rest of his family," NBC News wrote, dismissing the scandal as they would continuously do for years in defending

Biden. "There's no evidence of wrongdoing on either Biden's part, and Biden strenuously denied any foreign revenue streams from the debate stage."

As this book is being prepared for publication in 2023, we know much more about Hunter Biden's business dealings, and how Joe Biden's denials that he had ever discussed any of it with his son were always lies. We know that former Biden business partner Devon Archer testified to a congressional committee that Joe Biden joined Hunter's business partners on telephone calls at least twenty times. And we know that Joe had dinner with Hunter's clients at Café Milano, the swanky DC restaurant, right around the time Hunter demanded and received a $142,000 Porsche and accepted a $3.5 million wire from the wife of a former mayor of Moscow. We know that various Biden family members received at least $20 million dollars, in total, from foreign benefactors, routed through about twenty shell companies. We also know that Hunter sent threatening texts to a Chinese businessman, claiming that his father was with him as they awaited a payment they felt they were owed.

But we would see then, as we did throughout Biden's time in the White House, that the media were in the mode of fully protecting Hunter, and therefore, Joe Biden. Most national reporters had their heads in the sand because they didn't want the charges against the Bidens to be true. And that's the way they talked themselves into dismissing the claims without ever investigating them.

23

 ## The Barletta Years Begin, and Another DUI
2013

Congressman Lou Barletta should have fired me many times. I started in his office as the director of communications in February 2013, and for more than two years, I frequently arrived at work already drunk, often kept drinking during the day, and more than once was unable to make it to the close of business.

There's a liquor store on the House of Representatives side of Capitol Hill that most staffers know about. I don't remember what time it opened every day, but it was early enough for me to stop there on my way into the Barletta office to buy my daily bottle of Jägermeister. Looking back, I'm amazed to say that on some days I returned to the liquor store by mid-afternoon to buy another one.

A lot of the time, I would stash the bottle in my car, which was parked in one of the staff lots. I'd walk out of the office conspicuously carrying a pack of cigarettes and a lighter so that my reason for leaving was obvious. And then, of course, I would rush to my car and throw down a few quick gulps of Jäger before having that cigarette (needed to return to the office smelling like smoke instead of booze, of course).

Sometimes if I had the smaller flask bottle of Jägermeister, I'd hide it in my desk and just conceal it in my pants pocket as I set out to have a cigarette. Those times, I'd just stop in the hallway bathroom for a quick pop on my way outside. I always made sure to carry strong, cinnamon flavored Big Red chewing gum, and I typically wore a lot of cologne (usually Grey Flannel by Geoffrey Beene).

In the first week of my employment with Representative Barletta, I attended one of the regular meetings of "House Republican communicators," which were scheduled gatherings of the communications directors from all of the GOP members' offices. The path from the Cannon House Office Building to the meeting room in the bowels of the Capitol Visitor Center was complicated, through tunnels and long underground walkways, and I'm quite certain I would not be able to find my way there today sober. It was even more confusing if you were hammered, which I was the first time I had to go there.

I sat through the meeting, pretending to take notes about the messaging instructions from the handful of presenters. When it was over, I wandered out into the entrance hall, turned a couple of corners and immediately found myself hopelessly lost. I decided to follow an exit sign and found myself out in the bright sunshine. I stopped, standing in the grass outside the US Capitol somewhere, and looked around to get my bearings. After a few moments, I believed that I knew which direction I should be heading, and I set off again.

"Sir?" a voice called. I stopped and looked around. A Capitol Police officer was approaching me on foot, just a few yards away.

"Uh, yes?" I responded. Drunk and lost was not the best way to interact with law enforcement on federal grounds.

"Did you just come out of that door?" he asked.

"I did, yes," I replied. "I'm not exactly sure where I'm going. I'm trying to get back to Cannon."

"Oh, you'll want to go that way," he said, pointing across the Capitol grounds. "And be careful what door you use to exit the building. You just set off the alarm."

I got moving as quickly, yet calmly, as I could, and got out of there. Not the most auspicious beginning to my Capitol Hill career—drunk, lost, setting off door alarms, and drawing the attention of the Capitol Police. What a way to start.

I eventually made it back to my desk and never mentioned the incident to anyone.

The Capitol Lounge, or "Cap Lounge" for the initiated, became a go-to Capitol Hill drinking spot for me. I don't remember what time it opened in the morning, but like the liquor store, it was early enough to accommodate my before-work boozing while still leaving me time to get to my desk reasonably on time.

On many days, my pre-work routine involved a quick stop at the liquor store for my bottle of Jäger (probably while illegally parked) and then a sit-down at Cap Lounge. These were the days when I was bringing my dog, Ollie, with me, and so I would leave him in the car while I drank for thirty minutes or so. Because of the need to leave Ollie in the vehicle, this kind of thing could only be done if the weather was cool enough.

I would sit at the bar near the front door, pounding a quick succession of screwdrivers—vodka and orange juice—which were what I drank in these morning sessions, watching ESPN SportsCenter and the CNN morning show on the televisions on the wall.

In this period of my drinking, I was intoxicated twenty-four hours a day, and maintenance of a certain blood alcohol level was of paramount importance. In fact, it really was the complete focus of every single day.

Though I kidded myself that I was effectively hiding my drinking, it's impossible to drink the way I was without people noticing that something was wrong. And since I was resigned to the idea that I would not be drying out any time soon, I had to concoct a plausible cover story to explain the worsening problem of my apparent impairment in the office. I searched the internet for medical conditions that have symptoms similar to those of intoxication, and came up with hypoglycemia, or low blood sugar.

I found it online and couldn't believe my luck. It was right there on WebMD.com.

"Confusion, dizziness, feeling shaky." Got it, got it, got it.

"Irritability, sweating, trembling." Check, check, check.

"Numbness in mouth which can cause slurred speech." YES!

"Passing out." That one could come in handy.

Having settled on hypoglycemia as a medical condition that I was going to claim to have, I went about setting it up, initially by dropping hints around my coworkers that I was experiencing certain symptoms. I'd get unexplained headaches or complain of dizziness.

I made a special trip to CVS to buy a blood glucose monitor kit—one of those small testing kits where you prick your finger and test a small drop of your blood for sugar levels. Even the best actors need the help of props every so often, right?

And for the final finishing touch, I added a plastic tube of glucose tablets that I also picked up at CVS. What good would it be to measure your blood sugar if you didn't have any sugar tablets to save you? I situated these conspicuously on my desk right next to my computer keyboard so no one could miss them. To add to the absurdity of it all, I even picked fruit flavored glucose tablets because I thought they sounded the tastiest, even though I had no intention of ever eating one.

I talked about these things in the AA meetings I continued to attend, and I came to recognize the inherent stupidity in what I was doing. Beyond the fact that it was destructive to myself and everyone around me, it was also a pointless way to approach doing what I craved. I drank to get drunk, but I had to pretend at all times that I was sober, thereby preventing me from actually enjoying getting wasted. In more lucid moments, I realized what a colossal waste of time it all was, but I never yanked myself out of the cycle.

While all this was happening and getting worse, it was still early on in my tenure with Representative Barletta when I made yet another serious error in judgment.

In July 2013, Dena went home to New Jersey for Independence Day without me, which left me alone in the Alexandria condo for a few days, and of course, I used the time to drink to my heart's content. Once drunk, I planned a rare trip to the condo pool and headed out the door. This is where my memory gets a little fuzzy, with gaps having to be filled in by the police and court records.

The clearest recollection I have is sitting on a lounge chair by the pool and deciding that I'd had enough sun for the day. As I made my way back to the parking lot, I saw a police cruiser sitting behind my car with its red and blue lights flashing silently. An officer was standing on the sidewalk nearby, writing on a clipboard and looking at the right side of my car.

I don't remember the details of the conversation, but thanks to the police report, I now know that I confessed to crashing into another car before parking at the pool. I participated in a field sobriety test and failed, and declined to submit to a breathalyzer test. Of course, I was arrested.

"While talking to [Murtaugh], he admitted hitting a vehicle and driving to the current location," the responding officer wrote in the report. "He admitted to drinking one beer an hour ago at his residence... He was unsteady on his feet and an odor of alcoholic beverage emanated from him and grew stronger as he spoke."

With the benefit of all that information, I can today pull fragments of memory and picture driving toward the pool and veering too far to the right, solidly striking a parked car. I remember being able to keep the car moving, though it was noisy and difficult to steer, and limping to a parking spot. I think I just decided to deal with the problem later and proceeded to the pool as I had planned.

When I had retained a lawyer, he had a look at the documents provided by the police and the court and concluded that I had really screwed myself by verbally admitting at the scene that I had been driving the car before the accident. He also noted that because the date of the offense was July 5, 2013, it was within five years of my first DUI, which occurred on July 28, 2008. This meant that the penalties would be more severe than if it had happened a mere twenty-four days later.

My lawyer, who was a wonderful guy who really tried hard for me, managed to get the prosecutors to agree to a charge of a second DUI in ten years, instead of five, which reduced the potential punishment somewhat. In the end, I pleaded *nolo contendere* in Fairfax County General District Court, meaning that I was convicted without admitting guilt, paid fines, and had my driver's license suspended for three years except for work. In addition, an interlock ignition device was to be installed on my car, which I had to blow into before it would start. As far as jail time went, the judge gave me ninety days in county jail, with eighty of them suspended. Quick math said I was going away for ten days, and I would remain on probation for three years.

After the judge accepted the plea, I was immediately taken into custody, and I surrendered my clothes, watch, and wallet, plus my good luck charm. They gave me an orange jumpsuit—yes, the classic orange jumpsuit—with "Fairfax County Adult Detention Center" stenciled across the back, and some extremely uncomfortable sandal-type plastic shoes. I was taken to my cell block and shown to my cell.

"Welcome home," said the deputy who deposited me into my cell. It was on the second level of a small area that housed nonviolent offenders, and mostly those who were not going to be staying too long. Everything was cement block and steel piping, and most everything was painted white. My cell had a bunk and a stainless-steel toilet and sink combination. By some miracle, I had been placed in a block with cells that were all singles. This was where I would live for the next ten days.

Once I got over the fright of being locked up, the experience was at least bearable. Though I initially felt ashamed around my fellow inmates, I quickly realized how irrational that was, since we were all incarcerated together. The cell doors were locked only during sleeping hours and we were able to mingle freely, read the paperback books that were provided, or watch the one common television.

We were assigned regular chores that rotated among the inmates and included such things as scrubbing down the showers, which, interestingly, were also singles like the cells. But mostly what occupied me was killing time. I read a steady string of novels—*Firestarter* by Stephen King is the only one I remember—and looked forward to one of the three terrible daily meals, which were often just a pair of baloney sandwiches on white bread with a carton of orange drink.

I also learned how to access the money that had been deposited in an account so I could buy food from the jail canteen. These items, mostly just snacks, would arrive once a day. Other inmates taught me how to make ramen noodles palatable by crushing them up and mixing them with water in the plastic wrapper they came in. This gave you a room temperature version of noodle soup that seemed like high living compared to the baloney sandwiches.

Other inmates simply ate the uncooked noodles like a crunchy snack and sprinkled the granules from the flavor packet on them to make them tasty.

An additional problem associated with my ten-day stay in the Fairfax County jail was that it would not end in time for me to go on a trip that Dena and I had planned long in advance. It was supposed to be a fantastic getaway for the two us to Greece—her parents' native country—and Italy, but I would still be serving the last couple of days of my sentence when we were scheduled to leave. Dena took one of her two sisters instead.

I don't recall what excuse I used for the Barletta office to explain my lengthy absence, though I know I wasn't honest about where I was going. I do remember that my jail time encompassed two weekends, which took up four of my ten days inside, meaning that I only had to account for a maximum of six workdays missed. More likely than not, I just took vacation days and hoped to keep it a secret that I had been the guest of Fairfax County for about a week and a half.

On the day that I was released from jail, with Dena overseas, my parents were the ones who picked me up. And I can remember one thing quite clearly: Boy, did I want a drink.

24

The Media Try to Bury Hunter's Laptop
October 2020

As mentioned earlier, it was less than three weeks before Election Day, on October 14, 2020, when the *New York Post* broke what we thought was enormous news about a laptop owned by Hunter Biden, the contents of which linked Joe Biden to the rest of the family's business of selling access to him. The emails strongly suggested that the elder Biden knew about, approved of, and possibly benefitted financially from some of the deals.

It was a colossal story, or so we thought, and it couldn't have come at a time when we were more desperate for a boost. On the day the *Post* story hit, the RealClearPolitics polling average showed Biden with a 7.2-point lead, 51.2 to 44.0. But if we were hoping to be able to ram the laptop down Biden's throat by using the news media, we were disappointed almost immediately.

Eventually, most outlets would get involved in suppressing the laptop story, but it was the social media giants who got the censorship party started. Twitter suspended the *New York Post*'s official account, silencing the oldest continuously published newspaper in the country, which had been founded by Alexander Hamilton in 1801.

Twitter explained that the *Post*'s stories violated its rules prohibiting "distribution of hacked material," even though there was no evidence that the information reported was the result of a hack. The social media network also blocked the ability of other accounts to share the *Post*'s original article, calling it "potentially harmful."

While Twitter was effectively playing goalie for Biden, Facebook announced that it would be squelching the story on its platform as well.

"While I will intentionally not link to the New York Post, I want be clear that this story is eligible to be fact checked by Facebook's third-party fact checking partners," Facebook spokesman Andy Stone posted on Twitter. "In the meantime, we are reducing its distribution on our platform."

Subsequent reporting by other news outlets falsely claimed that Twitter restored the *New York Post*'s account "within a day." The truth was that the *Post* remained locked out for more than two weeks.

For the social media channels to make it impossible to disseminate these news articles from a major publication was of obvious incalculable benefit to Joe Biden's campaign. I will always maintain that it amounted to egregious, intentional election interference on a gigantic scale, and unwarranted meddling at that, because no one had been able to question or disprove a single fact as laid out by the *New York Post*.

While that argument was raging, we pressed the national press corps to write stories based on the *New York Post*'s account, but there were almost no takers. Yes, Fox News covered the news of the laptop extensively, the *New York Post* did many follow-ups or sidebar stories, and James Rosen of Sinclair Television did some excellent work. But the rest of the corporate, allegedly mainstream, media were aggressively uninterested in the story.

In fact, the managing editor of National Public Radio, Terence Samuel, explained why NPR wasn't reporting on the laptop by saying, basically, that the network didn't care.

"We don't want to waste our time on stories that are not really stories, and we don't want to waste the listeners' and readers' time on stories that are just pure distractions," he said without evidence.

Incredibly, the stated policy of taxpayer-supported NPR was that it was not news that it was possible that foreign nationals had purchased access to a vice president of the United States through members of his family. It was also not news that it was possible that this former vice president, who was at that time leading the race to be elected president, was aware of the financial schemes, approved of them, and perhaps personally profited from them. NPR didn't know if any of these things were true or not, because its publicly expressed editorial position was that they were not worth investigating.

This was the attitude of most everybody in the national media. So, the point of telling this part of the campaign story is not to relitigate the authenticity of Hunter Biden's laptop, which has since been confirmed as real by some of the same news outlets which refused to report on it originally. Rather, it's to show how utterly uninterested the media were in following a story that was harmful to Biden, and how readily they accepted the phony smokescreen that the laptop story was a Russian operation.

On CNN, two days after the *New York Post* story ran, there was an active discussion of the laptop, but only for the purpose of crushing the story. Former director of national intelligence James Clapper was a guest of Erin Burnett, and he let everyone watching know that if they believed the stories about Hunter's computer, they were being duped by the Russians.

"To me, this is just classic textbook Soviet Russian tradecraft at work," Clapper said without evidence. "The Russians have analyzed the target. They understand that the president and his enablers crave dirt on Vice President Biden. Whether it's real or contrived, that doesn't matter to them, and so all of a sudden, two-and-a-half weeks before the election, this laptop appears somehow, and emails on it without any metadata."

Three days after that, on October 19, 2020, Clapper would help to put that false explanation on paper with the release of a letter on the matter that bore his signature. The document, signed by Clapper and fifty other "former senior intelligence officials," was planted in *Politico* as an exclusive and claimed that the laptop story had "all the classic earmarks of a Russian information operation."

The letter also noted that there were nine other intelligence agents who, for security reasons, could not be named publicly, but were signing the letter anonymously, as though such a thing were possible.

The fifty-one (or sixty, if you count the anonymous ones) wrote that they each had "an understanding of the wide range of Russian overt and covert activities that undermine U.S. national security" and that if their assumptions were correct, "this is Russia trying to influence how Americans vote in this election." And they argued that the Hunter laptop story was "consistent with Russian objectives" and "key methods" that Russia has used.

They were forced to admit that they didn't have any proof of their claims, having not actually seen the laptop materials, but they were undeterred, mostly because they were impressed with their own credentials. They knew Russian behavior, they said, and their own combined "experience makes us deeply suspicious that the Russian government played a significant role in this case."

They closed with a declarative statement, just in case anyone missed the point: "It is high time that Russia stops interfering in our democracy."

The letter had the desired effect, though it has since been fully discredited as political dissembling and a piece of misinformation in itself.

News outlets, many of which had been looking for a reason not to cover the story, suddenly had something they could cling to. But with the days running out on the big digital countdown clock in the campaign war room, we kept pouring it on.

We peppered Biden with laptop jabs every day as part of our "Question of the Day" series, in press releases and tweets, which Jason Miller had instituted a couple of months earlier as a revival of something that had been used in the 2016 race. One question was, "It's been a week since new revelations of your son Hunter's foreign corruption and access selling have come to light. Why haven't you denied being 'the big guy' for whom Hunter is hiding foreign money?"

Another one read simply, "Where's Hunter?"

My comms team organized press conference calls every day for the final two weeks of the campaign, recruiting prominent members of the House and Senate to join us in hammering Biden over the laptop. I would emcee each call, getting in a few messaging points on the laptop issue before turning it over to the featured guest each time.

The senator or representative would speak for a few minutes and then we would open it up for media questions, which I requested remain on the topic of our press call—Hunter's laptop. Invariably, no one had questions on the subject and tried to ask about another campaign topic, which we would shut down. We wanted to talk about the contents of the laptop and how they related specifically to Joe Biden's fitness for office and whether he had been compromised by payments from foreign countries, including China.

We knew how many reporters were on these phone calls—plenty—and we knew that every day, exactly none of them was going to write the story we were beseeching them to write. Privately, several reporters told me that we were wasting our time, because "no one is going to touch it," in the words of one of them.

It's a difficult feeling to describe, but what ran through me during those closing days was something I would describe as enraged powerlessness. We could wail and harass, or nudge and cajole, and nothing was going to break through because the reporters had decided as a group, probably in an unspoken way, that it was simply not a story they were going to cover.

This was a perfect example of pack journalism, except in reverse. Instead of a gang of reporters all writing the same story, all with the same elements and spin, this form of groupthink involved everyone stifling the same story at the same time. In the view of the "cool kids" in the press corps, Fox News and the *New York Post* could have their fun, but the serious minders of the national narrative were not interested.

After the election, of course, there was evidence that the widespread blackout of the Hunter Biden laptop story had indeed helped the Democrats. President Trump's pollster, John McLaughlin, found that 36 percent of the people who voted for Joe Biden were unaware of the laptop story entirely, largely because they didn't watch Fox News or read the *New York Post*. And 4.6 percent of Biden voters said that they would have changed their minds if they had known about it, which was easily enough to flip results in swing states.

Once Election Day safely passed, news outlets began confirming the authenticity of the laptop. Over the next two years, *Politico*, the *New York Times*, the *Washington Post*, CNN, CBS, and NBC would be among those that verified the contents, and I don't recall a single quote from any editor who said, "Oops!"

In April 2023 it was revealed that Antony Blinken, Biden's secretary of state, had prompted the creation of the letter by the former intelligence officials which had raised the bogus specter of Russian involvement with the laptop. The former acting director of the Central

Intelligence Agency, Mike Morell, testified to the House Judiciary Committee that a phone call from Blinken triggered his decision to organize the effort to help Biden, because he wanted him to win the election. Further, it was hoped that the letter would give Biden something to use as a shield in a debate, which, as discussed earlier, was achieved.

I think it's worth spelling out explicitly what happened in this whole sorry saga. In the late days of a political campaign, Democratic operatives co-opted the authority and prestige of the American intelligence community to concoct the lie that Russia was behind the information contained in a laptop owned by Joe Biden's son. They painted an ominous picture of Russian interference in an American election to influence the media to suppress the story, a plan that successfully protected Biden from a scandal that could have cost him the election.

They lied to America that the Russians were interfering in our election, when in fact they were the ones doing the meddling. And one of the leaders of the scheme, Antony Blinken, was rewarded with the job of America's top diplomat at the State Department. In another time, perhaps with different candidates involved in the campaign, more reporters would be horrified by these facts, but that simply wasn't the case here.

What is most incredible to me is that, for the most part, the media simply didn't care, and I always believed that if a similar situation ever presented itself, most of them would make the same decisions as before. And as this book was being finalized, it indeed began to happen again following the launch of an impeachment inquiry in September 2023 to look into the Biden family's corruption. Many news outlets pre-emptively declared that there was no evidence, despite a mountain of known facts clearly begging for an investigation, and the cycle began to repeat itself.

25

 ## Getting Engaged and Going to Rehab (Part III)
2014

Dena and I had a little tradition that we tried to keep up, and that was going to New York City over Christmas. For our trip in December 2013, I had something special planned—when we got to the observation deck of the Empire State Building one night, I was planning to ask her to marry me.

The observation deck was crowded as always, and bitterly cold and windy, and it didn't feel like there was any way to be sheltered from the icy gusts. As we leaned against a wall, I put my head close to Dena's and told her I had a question to ask her. We had been ring shopping together, so it shouldn't have been a complete surprise. I'd discussed it with her parents, and they had already seen the ring. As she looked at me, I could tell that she had guessed what I was about to do, and I wasn't sure what her reaction was going to be.

I said the words—"Will you marry me?"—but she didn't answer right away. I had the ring out and everything, but it seemed that the transaction was taking a little while to go through. I could tell that she was conflicted, and who wouldn't be, in her situation? I knew she loved me, but I had not exactly shown her that I was in any way responsible, or that there was any guarantee that I would ever stop drinking for good.

I'd had many fits and starts, and I'd shown her that I was trying. And right there in the cold night air near at the Empire State Building, I was asking her to bet on me—to bet on me with the rest of her life. And she did.

There would be more days that would test her faith in the decision she'd made that night in New York. I would go for weeks without taking a drink, and then I would fall off. And sometimes they were bad falls.

There was a trip to Harrisburg, Pennsylvania, for a Barletta appearance at a local Chamber of Commerce breakfast, and I stayed in the Hilton the night before. When I woke up, I felt like crap, so I took a few pulls on my bottle of Jäger to knock down any chance that a hangover might settle in.

As I shaved, showered, and dressed, I had a few more drinks, so that by the time I made my way to breakfast in a ballroom downstairs, I was thoroughly buzzed. My only real function was to take pictures of the event and post them on the congressman's social media channels, and I set about doing that right away.

But after a few minutes, Barletta's district director approached and tapped me on the shoulder.

"Lou says you can take a break," he said. "Go up to your room and lie down."

"What?" I protested. "I just got here. I'm fine."

"You're not fine, you're drunk," he said. "You're out of the game. Go upstairs."

I didn't go into work the next day, but instead called Barletta's chief of staff to tender my resignation. I was told that the congressman wanted to speak to me, and when he came on the line, he surprised me,

SWING HARD IN CASE YOU HIT IT

"I want you to go get some help," Barletta said. "You go get better and come back to work when you're ready."

When the chief came back on the phone, I asked her not to be angry with Dena because I had worked really hard to fool her too, and she shouldn't be blamed because I kept letting everyone down.

I checked into Father Martin's again, and I could tell that my relationship with Dena was hanging by a thread. In a journal entry from January 30, 2014, the sixth day of my stay, I wrote that Dena had told me on the phone that we never should have gotten engaged. She said, understandably so, that it was a horror planning a wedding while her fiancé was in alcohol rehab and had no track record to indicate that he could ever stay sober.

She visited me a few days later, which gave me hope that things were salvageable, though she said that she only missed me when Ollie needed to go outside. She used words like "resentment" and "anger," and she said that she felt like her only choice was between canceling the wedding or going through with it and bracing for lifelong misery.

As Dena was expressing her raw feelings to me, I was coming to the realization that the only thing I had control of was my own behavior. Inside Father Martin's, it was emphasized that we can only fix ourselves, not other people. If we do what is right, other things in life will take care of themselves, one way or another. It's no guarantee of a happy ending for everyone, but it's a guarantee that there will be some resolution that wouldn't be possible if alcohol were still involved.

26

 **Election Day
November 3, 2020**

As Election Day approached, Dena decamped from Northern Virginia and took our two boys to her parents' house in Wildwood Crest, New Jersey. As a former campaign worker herself, she knew that the final days of any campaign are complete mayhem, so on a presidential campaign it had to be even more chaotic.

In elections past, it had been my experience that there wasn't a whole lot of communications work that needed to be done on Election Day itself, if you weren't traveling with the candidate. In other years, I had used the lull to get a haircut during the late morning and then have a relaxing lunch before getting ready for whatever evening event had been created to watch results come in. In 2020, however, that was not going to be possible because our candidate was coming to our headquarters for an update from campaign leadership and a little rally for the internal troops.

Shortly after noon, the president's motorcade rumbled to a halt outside our building in Rosslyn, which is a tightly packed hub of commerce, hotels, and apartments in Arlington County, Virginia, across the river from Washington. The streets of Rosslyn are jammed on a normal day, and the arrival of the leader of the free world did not exactly ease the congestion.

Trump had only been to the headquarters once before, because it was far easier for campaign staff to visit him at the White House than it was to move him around the Northern Virginia suburbs. In fact, I recalled hearing that when Brad Parscale had signed the lease for the campaign's office space, he'd had to reassure the building's management that the president was not expected to be a regular visitor. The implication was that the property managers didn't want other tenants hassled by the presence of a giant motorcade and Secret Service security measures, but there was also the undercurrent that Trump himself was not particularly welcome.

By that time in the race, the campaign occupied three entire floors in the building—the fifth, fourteenth, and fifteenth—with two television studios retrofitted on fourteen and fifteen. Nationally, we had about three thousand employees, paid by both the campaign and the Republican National Committee, and in my communications shop alone I had more than a hundred people. It was a hive of activity on Election Day when President Trump arrived.

First, he ducked into the main conference room on the fourteenth floor for an overview of where he stood in key states, and what the political team thought was likely to happen. The message he received that was it was going to be tight but that our Election Day operation was strong and that his people would turn out. We needed that to be the case, because we would be reliant on a massive Election Day vote to offset expected advantages that Biden would have when the early and absentee votes in the mail were tabulated. In the briefing, it was underscored for the president that it was going to be an extremely close election.

As the president exited the conference room, he made his way toward the area where he would speak, shaking hands and greeting the campaign staff as he went. When he passed me, he stopped and offered some praise for my work on television during the campaign.

"When we win this thing, we gotta get you over to the White House and head up some things over there," he said, repeating something he had mentioned several times before. "First thing is to win, right?"

I agreed with that sentiment and told him it would be an honor to continue to serve his administration in the White House. When he got to the spot where the press had assembled, Trump made some brief remarks to the campaign staff, some of whom were wearing masks, mostly for the benefit of the television cameras that were carrying the occasion live across many cable and broadcast networks. He was upbeat and optimistic.

"I hear we're doing very well in Florida," Trump said. "We're doing very well in Arizona. We're doing incredibly well in Texas. I'm hearing we're doing well all over. I hear the lines [to vote] have been amazing. I think we're going to have a great night, and much more importantly, we're gonna have a great four years."

He turned his remarks toward the campaign staff, whom he described as "young, attractive people that know politics," and said, "I want to thank everybody. It's a tremendous group of people."

As he prepared to take questions, he waved more of the staff over to get closer.

"Come on over here," he said, and then gestured to the reporters gathered. "This is the media, they're very nice and they treat us extremely well," he said to laughter.

In response to a reporter's question about the closing days of the campaign, Trump said he thought the nation could see that the economy was coming back strong and that his administration had handled the COVID-19 crisis well. He believed that the American people could see it, even if the media did not.

"I'm not sure that it's possible to convince you of it," he said directly to the media. "Because, you know, you people were not really convincible no matter what we did."

When asked if he'd prepared both victory and concession speeches, he said he had not, and had a moment of reflection that he shared out loud with the world watching.

"Winning is easy," he said. "Losing is never easy. Not for me, it's not."

After the president left, I saw one of our political guys—those folks whose job it was to know where the voters were and how to get them to show up. I asked him how he felt, and he said good.

"If I had to guess," he said. "I'd say we win in a close one."

I made a point of standing outside the door to my office, surveying as much of the campaign office as I could see from one spot. There was a steady buzz, some nervous laughter, and a general sense of high spiritedness. I said to Kimmy Hammond, my executive assistant, "I've been on winning and losing campaigns before, and this one just feels like a winner."

That evening, as polls gradually closed hour by hour across the country, the early returns looked quite positive. I began to receive text messages from friends inside and outside of politics, who sent early congratulations on what looked like it could be a great night for Team Trump.

And then at about 11:20 p.m., disaster struck, as Fox News called Arizona for Joe Biden, although less than three-quarters of the vote had been counted. We had known the state would be close and we sincerely felt that the Fox News call was extremely premature.

"@FoxNews is a complete outlier in calling Arizona, and other media outlets should not follow suit," Jason Miller tweeted at 11:47 p.m. "There are still 1M+ Election Day votes out there waiting to be counted—we pushed our people to vote on Election Day, but now Fox News is trying to invalidate their votes!"

In a second tweet two minutes later, Miller said, "We only need 61% of the outstanding, uncounted Election Day votes in Arizona to win. These votes are coming from 'our counties,' and the 61% figure is very doable based on what our other Election Day votes are looking like. @FoxNews should retract their call immediately."

Senior campaign staffers bombarded Fox News executives with phone calls, and Jared Kushner even called Fox chief Rupert Murdoch, all to no avail, and the network put the head of its "decision desk" on the air to defend its projection.

Biden took the stage before President Trump spoke to the country, telling supporters in Wilmington, Delaware, "We feel good about where we are, we really do," and, "We believe we are on track to win this election."

While Biden was talking, President Trump tweeted that Democrats were trying to steal the election.

At nearly 2 a.m., I again stood outside the doorway to my office and stared at the large television monitors in the mostly empty war room. It was a remarkable fall from feeling confident to realizing that victory was slipping away. What had seemed like a winning campaign just hours before suddenly felt like slamming into a brick wall after nearly two years of sprinting at full speed.

The congratulatory texts had stopped a few hours before and had been replaced by messages asking what was happening. By the wee hours of the morning, incoming messages had dried up completely.

As we awaited remarks from the president, it seemed like he had two options on how to play it—be conciliatory and talk about which possibilities lay ahead, or declare victory outright. Unsurprisingly, he chose to plant his flag. At about 2:30 a.m., President Trump finally addressed the nation from the White House.

"I want to thank the American people for their tremendous support, millions and millions of people voted for us tonight. And a very sad group of people is trying to disenfranchise that group of people and we won't stand for it. We will not stand for it," Trump said right at the top of his remarks, going state by state through the results.

Then he got to the part that vaguely foretold what the next two months would hold:

> This is a fraud on the American public. This is an embarrassment to our country. We were getting ready to win this election. Frankly, we did win this election. We did win this election. So, our goal now is to ensure the integrity for the good of this nation. This is a very big moment. This is a major fraud in our nation. We want the law to be used in a proper manner. So we'll be going to the U.S. Supreme Court. We want all voting to stop. We don't want them to find any ballots at four o'clock in the morning and add them to the list. Okay? It's a very sad moment. To me this is a very sad moment, and we will win this. And as far as I'm concerned, we already have won it.

By then it was quite late—well into the next day, in fact. I had a room reserved in the hotel right next to the campaign office, so I went and checked in to sleep for a few hours before returning to my desk bright and early the next day.

Election Day had passed, but there was much more to come, and no one had any idea what was still ahead.

27

 Married and Back to the Status Quo
August 17, 2014

When I got out of Father Martin's for the second time, in late February 2014, I got myself to an AA meeting that very night. I spoke up and told the room that I had just gotten out of treatment and that I was ready to surrender completely. For the next few months, my sobriety was hit or miss. Some days I could white knuckle through it, and other days I gave in to the cravings of the disease.

Dena and I got married on August 17, 2014, at St. Demetrios Greek Orthodox Church in North Wildwood, New Jersey. She was a member of the church, and we were allowed to be married there even though I had been baptized Catholic. But we almost didn't go through with it.

The week before the wedding, Dena had gone home to Jersey and was getting ready, when I decided to go out and get drunk again. Dena was aware of that, and she asked that we meet in a pizza place in New Jersey so that we might have one last conversation about whether getting married was truly a good idea.

I made the usual promises about getting my act together, and I truly did mean that I wanted to. Whether I would or could was another question, and one that I had yet to answer satisfactorily. I was pretty sure that she wanted to call it off, but I didn't, and I think the bottom line was that the ceremony was just a few days away and it would be horribly embarrassing to cancel it so late.

It was a long, traditional Greek ceremony, and at the end of it, we were married in the eyes of the State of New Jersey and the Orthodox Church. People cheered and loaded up in their vehicles to get to the reception up the road in Atlantic City.

After taking a ton of pictures, we went outside to board a trolley that would take us and the wedding party to the reception. Except there was no trolley. Somehow, two of my groomsmen had talked the driver into making a quick beer run to a nearby store, and they hadn't yet returned.

When Dena figured out that alcohol was the reason for the delay, let's just say that she was not pleased. The trolley eventually reappeared, and we all went on our way, but the ride was a little awkward after that.

The reception was fantastic, as Dena had planned a great party. The venue was a spectacular space that sat on a pier jutting out into the Atlantic Ocean. It was stunning and everyone said it was the best wedding they had been to in years.

Throughout it all, I could tell that Dena was less than completely happy, and there was even a sadness about her that she was trying to conceal. It was a lovely ceremony and party, but I knew that I was not the husband she had envisioned for herself, and I suspected that she felt that a part of her would always regret marrying me.

My ongoing behavior tended to argue that her misgivings were valid.

A few months after the wedding, I was making poor decisions again. Up in Hazleton for a Barletta work trip, I had gotten drunk and was sneaking a cigarette in the bathroom of my hotel room. When I finished, I flushed the butt down the toilet and opened the door, but enough smoke rolled out hugging the ceiling that it set off the fire alarm.

I didn't panic because this had happened a few times before in other hotel rooms, and I had always been able to remedy the situation by waving a towel at the smoke detector to make it stop beeping. This time, it didn't work, and I could hear through the door that the hotel was being evacuated.

I joined the stream of people walking slowly down the hallway and out the front doors of the hotel. Minutes passed and suddenly I could hear the unmistakable sounds of fire engine horns and sirens approaching, and soon a large ladder truck turned into the long driveway of the hotel property. Its lights were flashing insanely, and it made an awful lot of noise in what had previously been a very quiet night in this part of Hazleton.

The first truck was followed by a second, and then by an ambulance, and soon the entire front of the hotel was being streaked with zooming and spinning red and white lights. Thankfully, at least the sirens wound to a stop and the horns stopped blaring, and all that was left was the significant hum of the large engines that powered the emergency vehicles.

A handful of firefighters dismounted and strode purposefully into the building and were gone for a long while. As the minutes passed, I imagined what sort of forensic examination they were conducting that would lead them to my bathroom as the epicenter of the alarm.

Eventually, the firefighters emerged, climbed back aboard their trucks, and slowly rolled back into the night. We lodgers filed back to our rooms, and as I closed the door behind me, I allowed myself to believe that I had gotten through it and escaped blame.

As I looked in the bathroom once more, I saw that there were ashes in the sink. Clearly, I had tapped my cigarette there without realizing it, instead of ashing in the toilet like any good hotel room smoker should. I stood and quietly cursed myself, and then flinched with a start as someone knocked loudly on the exterior door to my room.

"Fuck," I whispered, and quickly rinsed the sink, washing the ashes down the drain like I should have done thirty minutes earlier. Opening the door, I found a male hotel employee standing in the hallway.

"Mr. Murtaugh?" he asked, verifying who I was. I confirmed it for him with a nod.

"We've determined that the alarm was triggered by cigarette smoke in this room," he said. "Were you smoking in here, or in the bathroom?"

I think I mumbled something non-committal.

"I just wanted to remind you that this is a completely non-smoking property, and that we will be charging you $250 for a room cleaning because of the smoke," he informed me. "You will see that charge on your bill when you check out."

He didn't say what I expected to hear next, which was that I was dis-invited from ever staying at the hotel ever again. Small miracles, I guess.

"Is that understood by you?" he asked, or some formal words to that effect. I confirmed that I had received the message. He wished me a good night, and I closed the door.

28

Post-Election Day
November and December 2020

There was a brief period after Election Day when I held out some hope that there were legitimate legal arguments that might put some of the states that President Trump had lost back into play. For confirmation that there was a chance, I looked to campaign manager Bill Stepien, deputy campaign manager Justin Clark, and campaign general counsel Matt Morgan. Stepien wasn't a lawyer, but he was a clear-eyed political pro and a realist, and Clark and Morgan were level-headed and honest attorneys whose opinions I trusted.

We held more press conference calls in those few days in the week of Election Day, with Stepien and Clark walking the press through our options and filings. But as the counting continued in states where the results were still not final, it looked certain that Joe Biden would be declared the winner at any time.

On Saturday, November 7, that's exactly what happened. The Associated Press called the race in Biden's favor—while Trump was at his golf course in Northern Virginia—by giving him Pennsylvania's twenty electoral votes, putting him over the magical 270-vote threshold.

While the proclamation that Biden had won the election spread around the various media outlets, Rudy Giuliani was, at that moment, in Philadelphia holding a press conference about a series of alleged incidents of voter fraud in Pennsylvania's election. This would forever be known as the "Four Seasons Total Landscaping press conference," and it gave birth to waves and waves of jokes on Twitter, sarcastic media pieces and opinion columns, and even its own Wikipedia page.

Giuliani and other Trump surrogates were in Philadelphia trying to draw media attention to the claims that the campaign was making in court, which included allegations of outright fraud, the improper banishment of our campaign volunteers from vote counting locations, and the unilateral changing of election law at the last minute without state legislative action.

But there was initial confusion about where the press conference was to be held. President Trump, obviously informed by the team on the ground in Philadelphia, tweeted that Giuliani would be holding the event at the "Four Seasons," which everyone took to mean the Philly location of the luxury hotel chain. But the president soon posted a tweet to clarify that the actual location of the press conference was a local business called Four Seasons Total Landscaping, in an industrial park far away from Philly's Center City district.

And that gave the media even more to ridicule. The event, held outside the landscaping business, was near two other enterprises that reporters loved to include in their stories: a crematorium, and a porn shop called Fantasy Island. The *New York Times* ran the definitive story about the incident under the headline, "Which Four Seasons? Oh, not that one."

The explanation, which was certainly plausible, was that the location had been chosen to get away from the crowds of protesters in

Center City, who had disrupted previous attempts to hold press events on the sidewalk. The business would be far from the street theater of the opponents, and the owners seemed to be receptive to the Trump campaign. But whatever the message of the press conference had been, the confusion over the name of the venue overshadowed everything and handed the media a ready-made reason to ignore the claims the campaign was making.

All in all, it was quite a Saturday. Biden had been declared president and Rudy Giuliani had held a press conference next to an adult bookstore. The post-Election Day phase of the campaign was not going well.

When I arrived at work the next day, a Sunday, someone had plastered photocopies of the front page of an old *Washington Times* edition all over the common areas of the fourteenth-floor campaign office. The headline blared, "PRESIDENT GORE" in capital letters, a clear message from an anonymous staffer to the rest of us that the media does not have a constitutional role in electing a president.

I had lived through the turmoil that followed the 2000 presidential election, with the court battles that reached the US Supreme Court, and saw a clear parallel to what we were up against twenty years later. I couldn't immediately recall a time when Democrat Al Gore had formally been declared the winner over George W. Bush back then, but the *Washington Times* front page was striking enough that I put that concern aside and took a picture of the photocopies.

I tweeted one of the pictures I took, with the caption, "Greeting staff at @TeamTrump HQ this morning, a reminder that the media doesn't select the President."

Before long, the *Washington Times* itself corrected me on Twitter, posting a message that read, "These photos have been doctored. The Washington Times never ran a 'President Gore' headline."

When I learned that the front page was fake, I was mortified because I had always tried to be truthful in everything I said on behalf of the campaign and was careful to limit my remarks to things I knew I could defend. So, the mild backlash that was happening on Twitter was disturbing.

I deleted the tweet without explaining why, but did tell the news outlet Axios that I removed it after realizing that the front page in the picture had been faked. The little episode spurred a flurry of stories across the internet, which just goes to show you how much scrutiny we were under the whole time.

It was around then that some research the campaign was conducting detected that some votes had been cast in certain states—Pennsylvania and Georgia, for starters—by voters who were no longer alive. We put out press releases detailing these obvious cases of fraud as an effort to open even the tiniest crack to discuss the possibility that the election had not been 100 percent secure.

The problem was that the media fact checkers went into over-drive to investigate the claims, and some of the deceased-voter stories didn't stand up under scrutiny.

Also at this time, our regular television appearances, which the president wanted to see us doing, began to get more difficult to manage as the legal landscape grew continually worse. We were pushing the fact that no state had certified a winner yet, and we were also critical of the way the election had been carried out in certain states. For example, we argued that some voters in Philadelphia were given the chance to "cure" errors they had made on their mail-in ballots, but people from other parts of the Commonwealth were not afforded that opportunity. That was disparate treatment, we argued. These were valid points, but a little thin on substance, and it was getting harder and harder to make it through a four-to-six-minute live shot without more ammunition.

On November 13, I went on Fox News with Jon Scott to answer for some court rulings that had gone against us in Pennsylvania. We had larger arguments that we were still optimistic about, but it was getting more difficult to project confidence when almost nothing was going the president's way.

Scott, with whom I'd appeared many times during the campaign, is the sort of guy who probably couldn't be rude if he tried. But he had no choice but to ask adversarial and challenging questions, because there I was still arguing for the possibility of success for Trump at that late date—ten days after Election Day and nearly a week after Biden had been declared the winner by the entire media, including Fox News.

This is how the interview started, with Scott's first question: "The appeals court in Philadelphia has denied five of your claims here regarding your campaign's claims there, regarding the election, meaning that those campaign, those votes are going to stand. Your reaction."

He continued with: "But according to the official count, Joe Biden leads in Pennsylvania by more than 60,000 votes. Are you thinking that you can overcome that margin in Pennsylvania?"

He followed that up with a piece of videotape, which he led into this way: "George Washington University Professor Jonathan Turley says so far he's seen no signs of inaccuracies or fraud or other problems in this election. Listen."

After I had run through all the low-probability arguments we were making, I was again careful to only say things that I knew we were alleging in lawsuits that had been described to me as legitimate by the lawyers I trusted. And at the end I got back to the one line that I knew was totally safe and inarguable.

"The idea is that we want to count every legal vote and not count the illegal votes," I said as we wrapped it up.

By mid-November, Rudy Giuliani and a campaign lawyer, Jenna Ellis, were trying to assert their dominance and were clearly more comfortable making more aggressive claims of fraud and abuse than the lawyers that had preceded them. I can remember being in a meeting in our main conference room with Bill Stepien, Justin Clark, Matt Morgan, and some others, along with Giuliani and some of his crew. Giuliani was talking about voting machines and fraud, the details of which I don't recall today, although I remember thinking that I wouldn't be able to defend it all on television if called on to do so.

As time ticked by, I saw Stepien get up and leave the room. After a few minutes, he was followed by Clark, and then Morgan. The meeting continued without them. After a long enough time had passed to convince me that they weren't returning, I got up and walked down the hall to Stepien's office, which is where I found them all.

The interior walls of the Trump office space were all glass, so I could see them all in Bill's office laughing and shaking their heads. I opened the door and joined them as they recounted some of the crazy theories we had just heard. We laughed together for a few moments before there was a sharp rapping on the glass wall of the room.

Jerking our heads to the sound, we saw Mayor Giuliani on the other side of the glass. He threw up his hands in a gesture of frustration and yelled, "Come on, guys, this is important stuff!" It came through the glass muffled, but we could still understand him.

Now that I think about it, that was probably the point at which I knew for sure that all hope was lost. Whatever was left of the organization I had joined almost two years earlier, it was coming apart at the seams, and it was only getting more frustrating.

Once, during a public event challenging the election results in Pennsylvania, Giuliani claimed that significantly more mail-in votes were counted in the 2020 election than there were ballots that had been requested. Such a thing should not be possible, but he claimed that it had happened.

Media picked up on this charge, of course, and wanted an explanation for how the mayor had arrived at that conclusion. Specifically, he said that only 1.82 million absentee-by-mail ballots had been requested by voters, but that 2.5 million votes had been cast by mail. If he was right, it meant that about 700,000 more votes had been counted than should have existed. Again, it should not have been possible, and the media wanted to know where those numbers had come from. So, they asked me, and I had no idea.

Since I had no insight into it, I forwarded the inquiries to Jenna Ellis and asked if she had an answer for the discrepancy. She explained that the mayor had supplied the numbers, which he said he had gotten from the Pennsylvania secretary of state's website, but that the data had been removed from the site since then.

I decided to do a little sleuthing myself by looking at that same website. What I found was shocking and maddening at the same time. According to the data, it looked like Giuliani had stated the number of mail-in ballots requested in the *primary* election (1.82 million), and then compared it to the number of votes cast by mail in the *general* election (2.5 million). Quite obviously, those were two separate and distinct elections—a primary and a general—and the two numbers were not relevant to each other at all. I alerted Stepien, Clark, Miller, and others to what I had discovered, and left it to Mayor Giuliani if he wanted to reply to any of the press asking questions about his math.

This madness was followed by a press conference at the RNC, the theatrics of which would overshadow the message that was intended to be disseminated. As the start time of the press conference neared, Jason Miller popped by my office and asked if I was going to make the trip up to Capitol Hill to watch.

"No," I said. "Maybe I'll watch in on TV."

And watch it on TV, I did, and stood aghast as I saw dark rivulets of fluid running down Rudy Giuliani's face on the screen. I remember getting closer to the television to see if I could figure out what it was, at first thinking that it was blood. It was widely speculated later, however, that it was hair dye running down in streams of sweat because the event was in a hot room. That press conference immediately assumed legendary status because of that, and it was generally agreed among the dwindling campaign staff that nothing else could happen that would surprise us.

29

The End of Everything
May 16, 2015

Everything in my life was building to a crescendo of alcoholic chaos, and I guess the only questions were how spectacular my disintegration was going to be and who else it would injure when it happened.

At the beginning of this book, I told the story of "coming to" in the Fairfax County lockup, where I learned that I'd been detained for public intoxication once again. A conviction on that charge would result in a violation of the terms of my probation and trigger an eighty-day stretch in jail, which would represent the end of everything.

Here's how I got there.

I'd been at home with Dena that morning, a Saturday, May 16, 2015, married less than a year, and I had been drinking already. We had had a fight, doubtless because I was stone drunk again, and I had stormed out of the condo.

Since I had no driver's license because of my most recent DUI conviction, I took a bus from a stop near our place and got off near a Chili's restaurant on US Route 1. It wasn't a place I had ever settled in for serious drinking before, but it was as good as any for that day, I guess.

The rounds I ordered at the bar were draft beers and shots of Jägermeister. The beer I would drink slowly, but the Jägers I threw down fast. After a while, I either decided that it was time to go or I was asked to leave by the establishment, and I attempted to walk home. I would not learn this until later, but I eventually meandered onto the grounds of nearby West Potomac High School—to find a bathroom, I theorize—where someone found me nearly unconscious, called 911, and summoned the police and an ambulance.

After I returned to relative coherence in the Fairfax lockup, as described in this book's introduction, I realized the depths of my predicament, and upon my release I contacted the same lawyer I had used before. It was a bad situation: I was on probation for a second DUI, I had eighty days of suspended jail time hanging over my head, and I had just been arrested for an alcohol-related misdemeanor. I was, in technical legal parlance, in deep shit.

But the lawyer came up with a plan. It was not guaranteed to work, but it was the best chance we had, and the end goal was to have the new public drunkenness charges dropped. It was the only way to keep me out of jail for nearly three months and the only way to avoid complete ruin.

If I went away for eighty days, I would certainly lose my job with Representative Barletta. Dena would probably divorce me. I didn't know which friends I could turn to, and I didn't know how long my parents would continue to put up with my act. My life, as I had known it and hoped it would be, would be over.

The only goal was to convince the prosecutor that I was serious about tackling my addiction, and that the Commonwealth was better off with me as a member of society trying to get better, than as a temporary inmate who would emerge from jail to return to a life that had been hollowed out.

The first thing I did was to voluntarily get the ignition interlock device reinstalled on my car. This would show the court that I was serious about not drinking and driving. I enrolled in an outpatient addiction treatment program in another part of DC, where I went to three evening classes a week and underwent urine testing at random intervals. Dena and I began volunteering at an animal shelter in Fairfax County, and I kept track of the hours to be able to report them to the court when I appeared on my hearing date. Finally, I participated in at least one AA meeting every day with someone at the Serenity Club initialing a spreadsheet showing that I had attended.

I provided all these materials to my lawyer, and on the day of my hearing, he had a ten-minute conversation with the prosecutor. He came back with the best news possible. The charges would be dispensed with by *nolle prosequi*, meaning that the prosecution would not proceed, but the Commonwealth's attorney did not want to see my name on his docket anytime soon.

It meant that there would be no conviction for public intoxication, and therefore no probation violation. I would not be going to jail for eighty days, I would not be losing my wife, and I would not be losing my career. It was such incredibly good news that I could scarcely believe it.

I felt like I had a new chance at redemption, after so many failed attempts to stop boozing over so many years. Like many alcoholics before me, the innumerable attempts at quitting had come in many forms, with many strategies and many motivations, but until that day they had all met with one result—a return to alcohol after brief periods of sobriety of varying lengths.

In the end, the thing that finally worked for me was being fully and seriously threatened—in a very real and tangible way—with losing everything. I had survived a scrape with it, but another misstep would mean that the legal system would crush me without remorse or negotiation. That got me sober, unlike anything else I'd ever tried on my own.

I had hit my rock bottom, and I was on my way back up.

30

When the calendar reached January 2021, almost no one from the original campaign team was going into the office anymore, unless they absolutely had to. For the few spokespeople left, there were still occasional television hits to be done. The questioning was difficult, even on the supposedly friendly shows, which is what often happened when you had a complete lack of good answers to give.

There was an issue coming up involving the concept of alternate slates of presidential electors from states where the campaign was contesting the results. Senior White House advisor Stephen Miller had mentioned it on Fox News the previous month and it created a little bit of media buzz. The idea, as I understood it, was meant to preserve the campaign's legal rights, should it ultimately prevail in litigation in one of the disputed states. For example, if the lawsuit in Pennsylvania succeeded and Trump was declared the victor there by the courts, he would need to have a slate of electors ready to cast their votes for him when the Electoral College met. If the deadline had passed for selecting those electors, the president could find

216

himself in a bind with no one from Pennsylvania to vote for him in the Electoral College. As a logical proposition, it made sense, but as a plausible outcome it seemed awfully far-fetched to me, admittedly as a non-lawyer.

The absolute deadline for action seemed to be Wednesday, January 6, 2021, when Congress would meet to count the electoral votes and declare a winner in the election. Vice President Mike Pence had a role to play, according to the vague theories I had heard, but before any of us went on television again, we had to have some idea of what was expected to happen.

In an email exchange with campaign consultant and Giuliani lieutenant Boris Epshteyn, campaign advisor Jason Miller and I tried to extract some information about the plan, but it didn't seem like folks on Giuliani's team were ready to share the details, if they even knew them.

"Some guidance on the Jan 6th scenario with the VP would be very helpful," I wrote to Jason and Boris. Jason chimed in that he needed some information as well, and how it related to what the "end game" of the effort looked like.

Boris responded that Giuliani wanted to keep the finer points of the plan under wraps for as long as possible, and suggested a bland, one-sentence statement that was an obvious dodge and didn't come close to explaining the anticipated mechanics of the process.

"Dude come on," wrote Miller. "Boris what would you say to Martha [MacCallum of Fox News] if asked on-air?"

"What I have been saying is [that] January 6th is the first date of significance and it is vital that the only electors counted are those who represent the most legal votes," Epshteyn responded. "If she goes into details, [we] would say that the Constitution, under the 12th Amendment, gives the Vice President significant power in terms of counting and selection of electors."

Miller shot back: "Yeah, there's no chance we'll be able to hide on the 1/6 play—I couldn't even hide it on the radio this AM! It's going to get discussed this week, so let's tighten up our game plan."

This difficult period raised a question for me that had been bouncing around in my head for many weeks by that point: What was I still doing there, working on a campaign that was really no longer a campaign, but a legal effort?

For one, I still believed in President Trump and the policies of his administration, and I felt a loyalty to the Make America Great Again movement as a whole. Additionally, I had been entrusted with the job of communications director on the president's re-election campaign—the most watched political campaign in world history—had held the position for twenty-four months at that point, and had always intended to see it through to the end. It was difficult to contemplate walking away.

Financially, it was a reality that if I quit abruptly, it wouldn't be long before I needed a paycheck again, and I wasn't sure who would be willing to hire me. Because President Trump had become such a lightning rod, it didn't seem likely that someone from his orbit would find much success in the mainstream private sector. On the political side, a presidential campaign was just ending and there wouldn't be significant political communications work available for a while.

And finally, there were the few younger staffers who remained on payroll. Another staffer had told me a few weeks earlier that the few junior employees left were looking to me as a guide for what they should do themselves. While most of them needed the paycheck also, I was told that they'd all resign if I did. So, I felt that I owed it to them to stick it out.

That's a long explanation to say that I felt like there wasn't much choice but to survive it all.

I made a rare trip to the office on the morning of January 6, 2021, because I had a television hit with Stuart Varney on Fox Business scheduled for about 10:15 a.m. I desperately didn't want to do anymore media appearances, but Stuart was a good guy, and I was okay with what the topics were going to be.

He started off by asking about the two elections for the US Senate that had taken place in Georgia just the day before. In an unusual occurrence, both Senate races had gone to runoff situations and both Democrats ended up beating their incumbent Republican opponents. Jon Ossoff beat Senator David Perdue by a count of 50.6 to 49.4, and Raphael Warnock defeated Kelly Loeffler by 51 to 49. Those two victories handed control of the US Senate to the Democrats.

In focusing on the runoffs, Varney wanted to know why Democratic turnout had increased compared to the November election just two months earlier, while Republican vote totals had dropped. I blamed the controversial issue of $2,000 COVID-19 stimulus payments to people and the public perception that Republicans in Washington were against them, but I privately agreed with Varney's implication: that consistent complaints about the 2020 election had discouraged our voters from showing up at the polls again so quickly.

Varney then turned to the large rally that was planned in DC later that morning, where President Trump was expected to speak. The big gathering was not sponsored by the campaign, so I didn't know a whole lot about it, just that it was happening, and that the president would be there. Varney asked me what the president was going to say, which I didn't know for sure, so I just gave him the regular rundown of election irregularities that I thought I could list with a straight face:

> I think he will run through all of the states that have been at issue here. Problems in states like Georgia, which I just mentioned. In Pennsylvania, how the secretary of state and the Democrat

Supreme Court in Pennsylvania effectively moved the date of the election by pushing the deadline to receive ballots by three days. The fact that, if you voted in Philadelphia, or if you voted in a more rural county, you were treated differently. In Philadelphia, you were given a chance to cure your ballot so that it wasn't kicked out if you had filled it out incorrectly by mail. In rural counties, you were not given that opportunity. So, I think the president will methodically go through the states where he sees that there were electoral problems, irregularities, and the fact that voting rules and voting laws were changed, in many cases at the very last minute, by bureaucrats and not the state legislature, as the Constitution intended.

That was the end of it, and Varney wrapped it up.

"Tim Murtaugh, thanks for joining us, sir," he said. "We hope to see you again."

That turned out to be the last TV hit I ever did on behalf of the Trump 2020 campaign, but I didn't know it at the time. I took my jacket, shirt, and tie off, changed back into casual clothes, and headed out, arriving home in Alexandria before noon, I think.

Later, I was lying on the couch reading a Jack Reacher novel when I received a text from Dena, who was upstairs in our bedroom.

"Are you watching TV?" she wrote.

I grabbed the remote control and turned the television on, and the first images I could process were of hooligans milling around in what appeared to be the US Senate chamber.

"What the fuck?" I said quietly. I had no facts about what had transpired, but I had a suspicion. I opened Twitter on my phone and started scrolling, and the sequence of events came into focus. It speaks to how completely tuned out I was by then that I had not watched one second of the rally and had been completely unaware of the assault on the US Capitol until it was well underway.

I texted Jason Miller, "This is insane."

The rest of the day was consumed with watching the news coverage, interspersed with phone calls and text conversations with the remaining campaign team, which included only a half dozen or so by that late date. The president weighed in from time to time on Twitter with messages that were met with outrage from the media, including one directed at Vice President Pence. At some point, Miller told us that no one from the campaign would go on television for the rest of the day, which was fine by me.

It was hard to fathom that the video of a writhing and seething crowd was actually taken outside the Capitol of the United States. It was more like something we'd see from some other nation with a far less stable form of government. We would learn later, of course, that in some locations, the police opened doors for the protesters, but that did not negate the scenes of actual violence we saw. We also would come to realize that the overwhelming majority of the people who had assembled for the rally did not walk to the Capitol or enter the building, but the people who were causing the mayhem were, to me, impossible to excuse.

It was enraging to see the footage of the people meandering through the interior of the Capitol building. Some almost seemed touristy, and a little bit surprised to find themselves in the places they were walking through, but I didn't find them amusing. Contrary to some conservative reactions I was seeing on Twitter, I did not view them as patriots, or heroes of the Trump cause, or daring symbols of MAGA. They were dangerous trespassers, and I thought they were doing more damage to conservatism than any Democrat could ever do, because they were personally validating every cartoonist stereotype the rabid Left had ever concocted. In short, they made every Trump supporter in America look bad.

I felt alternating senses of dread and sadness, because these were supposed to be serious places, the rooms of the United States Congress, where the greatness of American representative democracy was put to work. The invaders were completely out of place and did not belong, and as someone who had spent an entire career in political campaigns, I saw it all as desecration.

By the evening, I think those of us left on staff were all shell-shocked by what we had seen on television and couldn't even begin to understand how far-reaching the events of that day would be. We didn't know yet that President Trump would be impeached (and acquitted) again because of it, or that there would be a formal congressional inquiry that would ensnare many of us who had worked on the campaign.

We didn't know much yet about Ashli Babbit, the thirty-five-year-old woman who was shot and killed by US Capitol Police while she tried to climb through a broken window outside the Speaker's Lobby. And we didn't know about Brian Sicknick, the Capitol Police officer who died the next day after suffering two strokes. Those two cases, and others, would fuel angry debate for years to follow, but we didn't know about any of that yet.

I tried to process where I placed President Trump in all of this. I had not watched the rally or his speech, but by nighttime I had read excerpts and seen clips, so I knew the gist of his message. It had been, unsurprisingly, focused on his view that the 2020 election was stolen, and the anticipated electoral vote counting to come that day in Congress.

I strongly felt at that time, and still do, that the people who committed acts of violence, who invaded the Capitol, and who caused damage to federal property were responsible for their own behavior. It seemed to me that accusing a third party, like President Trump, of being responsible for the actions of independent individuals he didn't even know is antithetical to what should be an innate concept of personal responsibility. In sum, I think that people who singularly blame Trump are excusing those who committed crimes, but I can't deny that I was disappointed that the president had not attempted to calm the rioters more forcefully.

Two of the more senior communications people who were still on staff texted me that night and asked if we could all get together on a call. Matt Wolking and Zach Parkinson wanted to band together with me to resign from the campaign as a group. I respected and liked both of them, personally and professionally, and I took their idea seriously. I admit that I was tempted to join them because I thought it represented freedom from the insane pressure that had engulfed us all for so long.

I heard them out and kicked the idea around thoroughly with them before I gave an answer. It would be a symbolic gesture, certainly, because the new president would be sworn in just two weeks later, and I explained to them the sequence of thoughts I had already walked myself through earlier.

I talked about my feelings of loyalty to the president and dedication to the job I had signed up for. I mentioned the real problems of future paychecks and employment possibilities—the Left would always hate us, but could we afford to alienate the Right as well? And I told them about the younger staff, who would resign if I did, and I said I didn't want to compel them to quit. I told Wolking and Parkinson that they should do what they thought they should do, but that I would politely decline to be involved.

I feel I must note that I do not view a recounting of this conversation as a violation of trust, because it was already the subject of testimony in the January 6 Committee proceedings, and so it is already a matter of public record. In the end, none of us resigned.

Something else that was put on the record by the committee was a text exchange a few days later, in which Wolking, Parkinson, and I were venting about the president's silence on the death of Officer Sicknick.

"[S]hitty not to have even acknowledged the death of the Capitol Police officer," I texted to them.

"That is enraging to me," Wolking replied. "Everything he said about supporting law enforcement was a lie."

The January 6 Committee later made a big deal about this, but did not provide the context that this conversation occurred during the time when the media was reporting on Officer Sicknick as though he had been beaten to death by the mob. It was only revealed later that he had died the next day of natural causes.

We all officially went off payroll on January 15, 2021, which for me was almost exactly twenty-four months after I walked through the front door in the first place. I had taken a mighty swing at the biggest pitch of my professional career—the chance to win a presidential election—and missed.

Top Democrats made it clear that anyone who had ever been associated with the Trump administration or campaign would be considered unwelcome in polite society moving forward. House Majority Leader Steny Hoyer expressed support for a permanent blacklist, whereby no one who had ever worked for President Trump—even before January 6—could be absolved of that sin.

"None of the Trump officials who have resigned their posts over the past few weeks will salvage their reputations by doing so," Hoyer said. "They have all been a part of, and enablers of, the most dysfunctional, corrupt, and destructive administration in history. They should all live a life of shame for what they have done to our beloved country."

I had previously held Representative Hoyer in fairly high regard, especially for a Democrat, but this statement was so far outside the bounds of what politics should be that it really affected me. This wasn't a condemnation of what happened on January 6, it was a direct and unambiguous denunciation of any American who had dared to work for or support President Trump at any point in the previous six years.

It's often said that Donald Trump has an amazing ability to take the attacks that people level against him and make it seem like it's really his supporters who are the target. "They're coming after you, and I'm just the one standing in the way," is the way his pitch goes. It's often hyperbole, but it's effective and creates an "us against the world" mentality among the faithful. And it's that mindset that helped to instill personal loyalty to Trump among certain voters at a level that was probably never seen before in American politics.

But Steny Hoyer's statement proved that, at least sometimes, Trump was exactly right that his political enemies are also gunning for his supporters on a personal level. And even on the days when I might have been tempted to let myself drift away from Trump, attitudes like Hoyer's served to drive me right back into his camp.

31

 **Freedom**
May 16, 2015

It sounds cliché, but it truly did feel like a giant weight had been lifted from my shoulders when my legal picture cleared up. I would still be on probation until 2016, but as long as I stayed out of further trouble, the eighty days in jail would not be crashing down on me because of my Chili's adventure. I had not had a drink since the last arrest for public intoxication, so that fixed my "sobriety date," as it's called in AA, as May 16, 2015.

Most everyone who quits drinking has a specific reason to do so, and the ones who tried to quit many times before they succeeded can often pinpoint what it was that finally broke through. For me, I needed to be faced with utter devastation, both personally and professionally. That's the only thing that did it: the knowledge that if I didn't stop drinking immediately and permanently, life as I knew it would be over and unrecoverable.

As an alcoholic newly in recovery, I went through plenty of difficult situations, and I was tempted many times, but I never relented. I was present in all manner of places where alcoholic drinks flowed, and I never so much as snuck one. It wasn't always easy.

While it may sound strange to someone who isn't an alcoholic, I came to rely on the Serenity Prayer. It's very simple:

God, grant me the serenity to accept the things I cannot change,
The courage to change the things I can,
And the wisdom to know the difference.

In those moments when I was severely tempted to find a way to excuse taking a drink, I would stop what I was doing and force myself to recite that prayer. Boiled down, to me it means that the act of taking a drink, or not taking a drink, is something that I can control. And since I now know that, I can act on that knowledge and make the right choice.

One of the principles taught at Father Martin's is the concept of doing the next right thing. It doesn't have to be a major decision, and it doesn't have to be something that immediately affects your sobriety. It's just whatever is coming up next for you—when you have to make a choice, no matter how minor, make the right one.

For example, if I were walking across campus at Father Martin's and saw trash on the ground near a garbage can, the right thing to do would be to pick it up and throw it away. So, I would consciously make the decision to bend over and pick up the litter. It's about building habits and good muscle memory in your behavior.

For me, it was also about biting off chunks of sobriety time that I could chew. On the first few days after May 16, 2015, I did it a day at a time, and sometimes it was a lot less than that. Sometimes I'd wake up in the morning and say, "Let's see if I can get all the way from home to my desk at work without stopping to buy booze." And then I'd accomplish that.

Then I'd say, "Let's see if I can make it all the way to lunchtime without sneaking out to Cap Lounge for three to five drinks." And I'd accomplish that.

And so on, until I was driving all the way home and getting inside the door without stopping at an ABC store for Jäger.

One sober day turned into two, and then a few, and then weeks and months. I had unusual feelings of pride when I talked to people at work or socially, and I wondered if they could notice how sober I was. But then I dismissed that as silly because no one really notices sobriety. It's the drunks who stick out.

Eventually, I got to the point where I just saw myself as someone who does not drink alcohol. If drinks were offered to me, I'd politely decline because that just wasn't something I was interested in. Sometimes I'd say something like, "Oh, there's not enough booze here for me if I get started," and leave it at that, and other times I'd just say, "No thanks." I developed the mindset that I would sooner jump off the roof of a tall building than take a drink. Either act would have basically the same net effect.

Once that switch was flipped, it got a lot easier for me.

Things with Dena were improving, as one would hope a marriage would if one of the parties stopped being drunk all the time. From my perspective, it was nice not to lie constantly, but in Dena's mind I'm sure she was still questioning her decision to go through with the wedding. Even though I had finally quit drinking, nothing would ever change the fact that I had been an active alcoholic throughout our courtship and the first nine months of our marriage.

But as my sobriety continued, I hoped that I was regaining her trust day by day, so that we could truly rebuild and move forward. I know that I might be a jackass from time to time, but at least I could say that it wasn't being fueled by alcohol any longer.

32

The January 6 Committee
2022

A year and three months after the 2020 Trump campaign ended for me, it was brought back to life by a text message I received in the first week of April 2022 from an investigator from the January 6 Committee. Officially named the United States House Select Committee to Investigate the January 6th Attack on the United States Capitol, I saw the committee as a Democratic vehicle for trying to hound President Trump from political life.

"The Select Committee's investigation has revealed evidence of your involvement in and knowledge of events within the scope of the Select Committee's inquiry," read the text I had received from someone who identified himself as investigative counsel. "I am contacting you to see if you are interested in speaking with the Select Committee voluntarily."

I had followed the work of the committee through the media, and I believed that its members were on a strictly political mission and completely uninterested in any facts that contradicted the conclusion that they had already drawn. I spoke to many fellow Republicans, a lot of them veterans of the 2020 Trump campaign, who felt the same way I did. We could not defend Trump's every action, but the way his political opponents refused to relent in their pursuit of him made us reflexively protective of him.

Early Republican objections about the January 6 Committee focused on its creation and composition after House Speaker Nancy Pelosi, a Democrat, rejected two Republicans—Jim Jordan of Ohio and Jim Banks of Indiana—who had been selected by Minority Leader Kevin McCarthy. McCarthy, the top Republican, responded to Pelosi's obstinance by withdrawing all five of his Republican members.

The result was that the ultra-partisan committee would have only two Republican members, chosen by Pelosi, who already happened to agree with the majority Democrats on every point they would be "investigating." Representative Liz Cheney of Wyoming at first, and then Representative Adam Kinzinger of Illinois later, would be those members, whose main value to the endeavor was lending the whole thing a false veil of bipartisanship. Cheney, in fact, had openly discussed her own personal goal, even before the committee began its operations.

"I will do everything I can to ensure that the former president never again gets anywhere near the Oval Office," she told reporters in May 2021 after she had been ousted from her position as conference chairwoman for the House Republicans. After joining the January 6 Committee, she would be promoted to vice chair of that panel in September of that year.

Many Republicans like me might have been more open to the idea of a congressional inquiry into the events of January 6, 2021, had there been a more legitimate means created of going about it. The images of the people who had stormed the Capitol were still with me, and I cringed to think about the damage done to the nation and to the esteem in which it is held by freedom-loving people around the world. I believed that a full and accurate accounting of what happened and what went wrong with security was warranted.

But that's not what the January 6 Committee had in mind. As it was constituted, the committee was flagrantly partisan, with pre-conceived conclusions that were guiding its work. The committee members had already decided that President Trump was person-ally and singularly responsible for the events of that day, and they were merely working backwards from there. There were no dissent-ing opinions or alternative points of view among the members of the committee. There were only spotlight seekers who had opposed Pres-ident Trump before the election and continued their offensive even after Election Day had passed.

Being contacted by the committee made me recall the weariness I had felt by the end of the campaign, which had stretched for two months beyond Election Day. And, since it was public record that I was working as a consultant for Representative Cheney's Republican 2022 primary opponent back in Wyoming, a strong candidate named Harriet Hageman, I thought there might be some extra motivation to put me on the hot seat. (Hageman would go on to completely destroy Cheney in the primary and then win the general election that Novem-ber, all with President Trump's endorsement.)

Not knowing what to do in response to the text from the investi-gative counsel, I asked around and was connected to an attorney, Ross Garber, who took my case and negotiated my appearance before the committee. It was agreed that cooperating voluntarily was the best course of action for me. I didn't think that I would be a very valuable witness anyway, as I had no personal knowledge of what happened that day at the rally or at the US Capitol.

As the day of my testimony approached, I began to feel a little bit nervous, not knowing exactly what the committee had in store for me.

We had agreed that I would be appearing remotely by web camera, with my attorney sitting next to me, which seemed less intimidating than an in-person appearance. But still, the committee wouldn't hold its first televised hearing until the following month, so I had no mental picture of what the ultimate infotainment production would look like. At a minimum, I assumed that the committee was planning to pull soundbites from its interviews for use on television, so I coached myself to approach it like a hostile appearance on CNN or something similar. And I made a note to try to be boring, so I didn't seem like a good witness to call for a live appearance at a televised hearing.

A couple of prep sessions with Garber were helpful. If I knew the answer, I would answer the question, tell the truth, and not guess or speculate. If I didn't know the answer, I would say so. I was as ready as I was ever going to get.

At 9:10 a.m. on May 19, 2022, I sat down in front of a laptop computer in an office near Capitol Hill, with Ross Garber to my right and a bunch of lawyers from the January 6 Committee on the screen. They told me that no members of the committee were present, though it was possible that some could appear at any moment (none ever did). The official transcript shows that the committee was represented by ten people during the interview, while on my side it was just me and Ross.

After the preliminary instructions and biographical questions were out of the way, they got right into it.

"Going to election day, did you have an expectation about whether or not President Trump would win reelection?" they asked me, according to the official transcript released by the committee.

"I can recall being advised by one of the guys that he thought that it looked pretty good, that it was going to be tight but that he thought we would win," I replied, thinking it was an odd question. "I mean, I think everyone goes into any campaign with the mindset that you're going to win."

"Was there discussion regarding the possibility that the president may be ahead on Election Day but that that number could change when all votes were counted?" a committee staffer asked.

"Our political team was very clear in that they expected the president's Election Day turnout to be huge, yes, and that the mail-in votes may tend to favor Biden," I said. "I think that was understood by everyone on both sides."

They focused a lot on the messaging that came from the president and the campaign that suggested that the election had been stolen, and they wanted to know if I'd known in advance what the president was going to say when he addressed the nation in the small hours of the morning following election night.

"Did you have discussions with anyone about pivoting to a 'steal' message post-election?" they asked.

"I mean, I don't recall any specific discussions of it. I think everyone was aware that that's the way that the President was framing it," I said.

"So is it fair to say that it was widely understood that because the President was claiming that there was fraud everyone else would also be claiming the same thing?"

"It is—look, a campaign is an extension of the candidate," I explained. "And I think any campaign from any political party would hold to that description. And I don't think that anybody in America who was paying attention was confused as to what the President's position was."

I tried to get the committee to see that cries of election fraud were not limited to President Trump, and I called attention to the obvious blind spot that they had for Democrats who had made similar claims in years past.

"The current White House press secretary has tweeted in the past that the 2016 election, where President Trump was elected President, was stolen," I said. "She has also tweeted that Stacey Abrams' election as governor of Georgia was stolen. And so I don't think that this type of messaging is something that was invented by the Trump campaign."

They brushed right past those arguments and continued on their line of questioning, eventually getting to Trump campaign claims that dead people had voted in the 2020 election. It was true that in the days after the election the campaign had released information about dead voters, and that some of it had turned out to be erroneous and the number of legitimate incidents cited had turned out to be very few.

"Do you have any recollection as to what the purpose of this exercise was, why the campaign was working so hard to prove that it could find people whose votes had been cast after they had died?" came the question, the answer to which seemed excruciatingly obvious.

"To publicize the fact that dead people had voted would be to draw attention to the fact that the election system is imperfect," I said.

"Is it fair to say that—to suggest that—to undermine a potential claim to victory by Joe Biden?"

"I think it is to—the effort all along, as we stated publicly dozens and dozens and dozens of times, was to make sure that everybody who is eligible to vote be able to legally vote and vote once and have it be counted," I said. "If there are dead people who voted, that obviously runs contrary to that. I don't think you'd find too many people who would be publicly willing to say that they support dead people voting."

Then they wanted to know why we had looked into the party affiliation of the alleged dead voters, and why we had wanted to publicize only the dead Democratic voters we had found. They seemed to think that the campaign should have been operating as a public news service, rather than as a political campaign.

"Look, this was a campaign to re-elect one particular candidate," I said. "Naturally, that campaign is going to be engaged, for the length of its existence, to promote things and ideas that benefit that particular candidate."

That seemed to sink in, because the interviewer responded with understanding: "Do you say that because here, the effort here is to show purely dead people who would've voted for Joe Biden and not for President Trump? Is that fair?"

Maybe this was the methodical process of questioning, but it felt idiotic to me.

"Again, I say, this was the Donald Trump campaign, and so I think it's expected that our efforts, whether it's on this question or a million other questions, are intended to benefit Donald Trump," I explained. "That's the way any campaign operates. There aren't very many campaigns who will conduct and publicize research purposefully to benefit the opponent."

And then it got almost comical.

"On its face, this appears to be pointing out that dead people had voted, which, of course, should not be possible," I said.

"Now, when you say 'should not be possible,' I mean, is it fair to say there's some level of fraud that's possible in any election? I mean, is that not presumed? There's no zero fraud in an election, right?" came the response.

"I think it's—it ought to be accepted as fact on its face that dead people are not capable of voting," I said.

"Well, to be clear, it's not a dead person voting; it's someone illegally casting a ballot on behalf of a dead person, right? So the theory is that, can someone illegally vote in an election? Which no one thinks is impossible by 100 percent. Is that fair?"

"It is clearly not impossible to illegally vote," I agreed. "Correct."

The press conference claims that Rudy Giuliani and attorney Sidney Powell had been making about Dominion Voting Systems machines were also on the minds of the committee staff, and we covered the fact

that the campaign had researched some of the allegations and found
them to be false. Since it came up, there was in fact an issue with one
of their press conferences that I wanted to clarify.

"Do you remember is there one press conference that stood out
more to you than other press conferences?" I was asked.

"There was one at the RNC that I recall, which was widely pub-
licized and made fun of [because of] hair dye running down Mayor
Giuliani's face. I remember that one," I said. "I remember the one in
Pennsylvania because it was held at the—for some reason held at the
landscaping company."

"That would be the Four Seasons Landscaping?" the questioner
wanted to verify.

"That's the one," I confirmed.

"So, let's go back to RNC—" They wanted to continue, but I wasn't
finished on that point yet.

"The campaign did not select that location, by the way," I said. "I'd
like that to be on the record."

"Duly noted," came the response.

It followed that we talked about the kind of advice the president
had been getting from his lawyers.

"I was of the opinion at a certain point, I can't say exactly when,
that Sidney Powell and Mayor Giuliani were not either giving the President good advice or saying things in public that I could personally
stand behind," I told the committee staffers.

And that brought us to a discussion of the Pennsylvania mail-in
voting statistics, when Giuliani appeared to have compared primary
election ballot requests with general election ballots cast. To me it was
different than other complaints I had heard, because I could actually
look it up.

"With regard to different claims [Giuliani's legal team was] making
about eyewitness statements and affidavits and different things that

were involved in whatever lawsuits they were filing, I would have no way of knowing the accuracy of the things that their witnesses were claiming," I said. "This is one of the only times where an allegation was actually researchable."

The interview felt long and grueling, but it wasn't without its lighter moments. At one point, I noted that the time on my parking app on my phone would be running out soon.

"Before we break, are you okay, Tim? Do you need a bathroom break or anything?" Ross Garber asked me.

"It depends how long we're going to—I have 20 minutes until I refresh my parking again," I said. "I'm okay."

"Should we go for another 20 and [take] a break when it's time to refresh parking?" someone from the committee said.

"That's fine," I agreed. "I hope I only get a ticket and don't get towed. You guys will cover that, right? Will you cover it?"

They laughed, but no one answered me.

We turned to the issue of the alternate electors, which was a plan to arrange for competing slates of Electoral College voters to rival Biden's electors in certain contested states. I had heard vague outlines of the plan but didn't have any firsthand knowledge of it. The committee cited an email chain from December 2020 that contemplated an aggressive media strategy, which it turned out was never employed. I said:

> My basic understanding, which again is very basic, is that a different set of electors was a good idea to preserve the campaign's rights should the campaign prevail on key litigation down the road. If the campaign won a certain case, and then we turned around and looked and there was no slate of electors that had been elected by whatever the deadline was, then that would cause a problem. That's my understanding, that it was all about preserving the rights of the campaign should litigation prevail. That's about the extent of what I understand.

The January 6 Committee staff were also very much interested in the many fundraising emails the campaign sent out in the post-election period, especially because much of the messaging of those solicitations focused on the legal effort that was underway at that time. Text at the bottom of the emails explained that a chunk of the donations would be directed to the president's political action committee.

Reporters had noticed this at the time and bombarded the campaign with questions about the fundraising appeals and the different buckets the donations would fall into. They weren't questions that the campaign ever answered.

"One of the first things you do when you receive a reporter inquiry, here, this period, post-election, or at any time, on any campaign, is you ask the question, 'Are we going to reply to this at all or not?'" I said, and explained that after discussion, the campaign had decided not to answer those questions. The reporters could wait until the campaign finance reports were filed and they could track the money that way.

The committee staff appeared to be genuinely offended by the Trump campaign's emails, and I questioned how broadly they applied their distaste for fundraising practices.

"I never really give fundraising emails much thought," I said. "I see a lot of fundraising emails come into my inbox today from all sorts of campaigns from across the spectrum politically—Republican campaigns, Democratic campaigns. Every one of them is written in a breathless [tone], as though, if I don't contribute right now, immediately, the world is going to end.

"So, if you're going to say that this committee believes that there needs to be 100 percent adherence to only the facts in fundraising emails, then I would say that you're indicting every single political campaign that exists today," I said.

It was painfully apparent that the committee was not engaged in a search for the truth. Instead, the staff were trying to coax sound bites out of me that they could use in their televised hearings. They tried at least eight separate attempts to extract a pithy soundbite from me by repeatedly asking me what I thought about Trump's public response to the Capitol riot. I just kept repeating that I'd wished the president had said more, until they tired of asking.

But near the end of my interview, I was willing to say at least one thing that they were looking for.

"And when [Trump] says that these were great patriots who attacked the Capitol, you didn't believe that to be true either, did you?" they asked.

"I don't think it's a patriotic act to attack the Capitol," I said. "But I have no idea how to characterize the people, other than they trespassed, destroyed property, and assaulted the US Capitol. I think calling them patriots is, let's say, a stretch, to say the least."

"Is that all it is, a stretch? Or just flatly wrong?" came the prompt.

"I don't think it's a patriotic act to attack the US Capitol," I repeated.

"Would you call it unpatriotic?"

"Criminal. Unpatriotic, sure," I agreed.

Before we finished, they made sure to remind me of the text messages that flew around among me, Matt Wolking, and Zach Parkinson. In one of them, in which I was critical of Trump's silence on the death of Officer Sicknick, I had said, "You know what that is, of course, if he acknowledged the dead cop, he'd be implicitly faulting the mob. And he won't do that, because they're his people. And he would also be close to acknowledging that what he lit at the rally got out of control. No way he acknowledges something that could ultimately be called his fault. No way."

By that, I had meant that if the president acknowledged the violence of the mob, the media would surely use it to place all the blame on him. And, having observed him enough, I did not believe that he would hand the media that opportunity.

Some of my text messages and an audio clip made it into the televised hearings. I was never called to testify in person, because as Ross Garber observed, I didn't make a friendly witness for the committee.

At 4:58 p.m., our interview concluded, almost eight hours after it began, and I left Capitol Hill mildly fatigued, but hugely relieved that the ordeal had passed. It had been an extremely political conversation, far less than a fact-finding discussion, which had been mostly dedicated to efforts to get me to express negative views of President Trump.

This wasn't an inquiry to find out what happened, to examine security lapses, or to analyze precisely where breakdowns had occurred. This was meant entirely to build a greater public record, for use in heavily produced televised hearings, to sway public opinion against Trump in case he ran for president again.

That's all the committee members were doing, and that's why, while I told the truth, I was glad to be a difficult witness for them. That testimony was the last real public act I performed for the 2020 Trump campaign, fully eighteen months after Election Day. It had to be the longest campaign in history, and many would agree that it has never really ended.

AFTERWORD

In the immediate aftermath of the campaign and January 6, I tried in vain to find a job outside of politics in the private sector. Like many others before me, I had spent decades in the campaign trenches, and had hoped for a real professional breakthrough after securing a senior position on a presidential campaign—especially one that's the re-election effort for the incumbent president.

To me, the principles of political communications are the same as you'd employ in selling any product. If I can help to market a candidate for office and navigate the terrain of a difficult campaign, I ought to be able to handle communications crises in private business. Many people who have held the top comms jobs on campaigns in both political parties—even the ones that lost—have been able to walk into high-profile public relations gigs in corporate business, tech, sports, and other private endeavors. But none of those avenues opened up to anyone from the Trump campaign.

It got so absurd that I was told by an oil and gas company, which had seen President Biden cancel a major project of theirs early in his administration, that it couldn't even consider me because of my association with Trump. That's correct—an oil and gas company was afraid to hire someone from the Trump campaign for fear that the Left would turn on them, as if the Left didn't hate oil and gas already.

The strange thing was that I had been doing political campaigns for twenty years before I worked for Donald J. Trump's re-election, but all that the detractors can see is the work I did for a president they can't stand. Nevertheless, I would do it all over again.

I'm proud to have worked for President Trump, both in his administration and as communications director on his re-election campaign. I would certainly rather that we had won the election in 2020, but we did not.

Despite the blacklisting pushed by people like Steny Hoyer, I found success after the election anyway. Working on political campaigns is what I do, and so I went into business doing exactly that, opening a firm called Line Drive Public Affairs. I had a very successful 2021 and 2022 with clients spread across the country, and in 2023 I worked with the consulting firm National Public Affairs (NPA), led by partners Bill Stepien, Justin Clark, and Sean Dollman—all alums from the 2020 Trump campaign, just like one of their vice presidents, Nick Trainer. After a year, I returned to Line Drive full time, but continued my association with NPA.

Along the way, other opportunities have presented themselves, ones I never would have seen had I not worked on the Trump campaign, and I have been grateful for each one. In addition to the candidates I've worked for in the years since, I've served as a visiting fellow for The Heritage Foundation and written a regular column on politics and the media for the *Washington Times*. I still regularly engage with many of the reporters I worked with daily in 2020, and I am always pleased when they tell me that I was one of the ones who emerged from that campaign with my reputation intact.

Yes, it's true that 2020 could have ended better, but even so, that campaign clearly advanced my career and raised my profile, and I have President Trump to thank for it.

SWING HARD IN CASE YOU HIT IT

Of course, there are some former colleagues from Trump World who have changed their minds about our shared former boss and have refashioned themselves into Trump critics. That's their business and I respect their right to voice whatever opinions they may have, but it is grating to see some of them preen in their new careers as anti-Trump Republicans. It's a little sad to see them appealing to the Left by emerging as critics of the president they once served, since everyone knows that the Left will never truly accept them because they will always be, in fact, Republicans who once worked for Trump. And it's baffling to watch them downplay their conservative roots and beliefs, of which they were once fiercely proud, in vain attempts to fit in with their new leftist media colleagues.

There are other former colleagues who went on to work for candidates other than Trump in the 2024 Republican primary field. That's fine, of course, because working for a candidate for a period of time should not bind you to that person for life. It struck me, though, that every time they attacked Trump on his record, they were attacking things they had once defended. As such, they would be slamming their own work as campaign operatives. That must be a difficult position in which to find yourself.

I still admire and respect President Trump and treasure the experience and memories I accumulated while working for him. I can't say that I agreed with every decision or statement he made, and I wasn't having the time of my life at every moment of the campaign, but he was my president, and I was proud to be on his team.

I would not have been able to follow my professional dream of running the comms shop on a presidential campaign if my wife Dena had not been there with me. We had two very young children while I was working long hours and traveling a great deal, and she shouldered a massive burden of keeping the kids alive while also working a full-time job herself. She sacrificed so that I could take my dream job, just as she sacrificed during the years when she was trying to keep me from destroying myself.

If you have read this book, you already know that I probably would not have lived to see the year 2020 had Dena given up on me. Against her better judgment, and against the advice of friends, she just didn't want to cut me loose. I'm not sure I would have had the ability to keep supporting a person who engaged in as much destructive behavior as I had, but I am eternally thankful that Dena did. She is a fantastic wife and wonderful mother to our two boys, and we all love her very much.

My parents and my brother Steve never knew what to do with me when I was so out of control, but I think that my father understood that I had to eventually find a way to stay sober for myself. Having been through it himself, I think he got it, and he and my mother helped to put me in situations, like rehab, where I had the most tools and the best chance of success.

My aunt Kathy was someone I talked to a lot when I was struggling, and my cousin Brian saw a lot of my antics in person, so I owe them both a load of thanks. My oldest friend, Mike Fisher, and his wife, Kristen, always showed genuine concern and offered straight talk.

Professionally, there was no one like Representative Lou Barletta, another one who just refused to give up on me. For the employers along the way who did fire me, or who declined to hire me in the first place, I understand completely why they did what they did. My behavior was frequently disqualifying, and their actions provided me lessons that I should not have needed to learn, and which I should have heeded much sooner.

My two children, who turned five and seven by the time this book was published, have never seen me take a drink, and I'd like to keep it that way. When they're old enough, I'd like for them to read this book and know that their father was a real idiot sometimes, but that he got better, and that it was their mother who helped to reel him back in. If that's all this book ever accomplishes, then I'll be happy.

And finally, I hope that if fellow drunks read this, they can connect with it in some way and maybe put off picking up a bottle for just a few more minutes while reading it. I know that in recovery, I am always just one drink away from reliving disaster, and the thought that my experience might help someone else helps keep me sober.

What I tried to do here, like my dad used to say all those years ago, was to "swing hard in case I hit it."